Full Circle

E L Black MA M Ed is Principal of Middleton St George College of Education and was formerly Chief Examiner in English Language for the Joint Matriculation Board and for the University Entrance and School Examinations Council of the University of London

F E S Finn BA was formerly Head of the English Department of Exmouth School

By the same authors

NEW ENGLISH LANGUAGE TEST PAPERS

MULTIPLE CHOICE TESTS IN ENGLISH LANGUAGE

Cover design by Craig Dodd

Full Circle

E L BLACK MA MEd
F E S FINN BA

John Murray   Albemarle Street   London

Acknowledgements

The authors are grateful to Mr C. R. O'Day for his help with the book lists and for his analyses of literature topics and questions. Also to the authors (or their agents or trustees) and publishers mentioned below the extracts for their permission to quote copyright material.

Thanks are also due to those who have kindly permitted the reproduction of the following copyright pictures:

'Strike Pay' (page 9) – Radio Times Hulton Picture Library; 'FA Cup Final' (pages 58–9) – Keystone Press Agency Ltd; 'Tube Station' (page 108) – London Transport; 'Joe Brown' (page 152) – BBC Copyright Photo; 'Trench on the Somme' (page 176) – Imperial War Museum; three cartoons (pages 36, 82 and 131) reproduced by permission of *Punch*.

Photoset, printed and bound
in Great Britain by
REDWOOD BURN LIMITED
Trowbridge & Esher

0 7195 3008 3

Contents

Introduction

This book is the result of the collaboration of two teachers – one of whom is working in the classroom, while the other is preparing student teachers for such work. Both have long had close connections with school examinations, the G.C.E. and the C.S.E., and have experimented with new methods of assessment, which range from continuous assessment involving projects and course work to multiple choice comprehension tests in formal examinations.

No-one wishes to return to the kind of English lesson which consists of sterile exercises in clause analysis and parsing, but it is clearly the English teacher's job to help his pupils to write correct and appropriate English that will not disconcert a reader by its ignorant errors, careless mistakes or unsuitable prepositions. Such a policy necessitates the use of some technical terms. There need be no apology, therefore, for bringing back the use of a few technical terms such as *adjective* and *noun*, for knowledge of such terms is an essential if currently neglected part of English. Anyone who receives letters of application for posts in industry and even in teaching cannot fail to realize that there has been a noticeable decline in standards of literacy. It is equally apparent in the daily press that the old standards of precision and correctness have been eroded.

Full Circle has been organized to provide work for all pupils who are aiming at an examination in their fifth year in a secondary school. While the two examinations, 'O' Level and C.S.E., exist side by side, it is almost certain that each teaching group will contain some pupils who will take G.C.E., some who will take C.S.E., and some whose future is still to be decided. The exercises in each Unit, therefore, range from 'O' Level standard to Grade 4 C.S.E. For example, the multiple choice comprehension questions are primarily for 'O' Level candidates, and the project work mainly for C.S.E. pupils. But the revision of punctuation, grammar and spelling may be necessary for all; in fact, this work may not be revision at all but, depending on the English syllabus of the school concerned, a first look at things without which 'good' English is impossible. If, as seems possible and reasonable, G.C.E. 'O' Level and C.S.E. examinations become a single examination, this book will be of use throughout the ability range of candidates. Until then, the exercises in this book may help teachers to make a decision – sometimes difficult – on the choice of course and examination for pupils, especially those who could be termed 'borderline'. Should a new examination, to be called the C.E.E., be introduced for sixth-year pupils who wish to improve on C.S.E. grades 2 to 4, this book should provide all the necessary material.

The teaching of English inevitably includes 'composition' – ranging from the formal essay to a short story, and requiring either imaginative or factual treatment. The other obvious and equally necessary ingredient of English is 'comprehension', which ranges from the testing of the understanding of the meaning of words to the appreciation of the style and content of both verse and prose. In addition to exercises, this book provides ideas and suggestions which should help any pupil of average or above average ability to add to his English experience.

Units 1 to 15

Each Unit is divided into three parts:

PART I consists of comprehension exercises, both multiple choice and traditional. The questions range in difficulty from good 'O'-Level standard to average C.S.E. The questions also vary in type to suit the different approaches of the two examinations. Generally speaking, it will be found that the objective questions are more suitable for G.C.E. candidates, whereas the traditional questions should not be beyond the ability of the majority of fifth-year pupils, especially if dictionaries are used, a practice common in C.S.E. examinations and very helpful in training pupils to discriminate between words of similar meaning.

PART II is the 'composition' section. Each Unit contains a wide choice of titles suitable for 'O' Level and C.S.E. candidates. In every Unit some titles are linked with the passage in Part I to provide assistance to the pupil who finds it difficult 'to get started'. Included in this section are Suggestions for Projects, Assignments and Course Work. Many of these could be used for compositions, but are mainly intended for extended project or course work in which research, note-taking, writing and illustrating might occupy a whole term.

PART III. All Units contain the following sections in Part III:

Punctuation. Suggestions for systematic revision, hints on overcoming difficulties, and exercises.

Grammar and Usage. Suggestions for the revision of parts of speech etc. helpful to the writing of good English, correction of errors, English usage.

Spelling and Dictionary Work. Revision of spelling, with reminders about helpful rules, exercises to train pupils to use dictionaries and to acquire an interest in words by directing their attention to derivations.

Style and Appreciation. This section covers a wide range of topics, from the understanding and explaining of figures of speech to the complete appreciation of poems and short prose extracts (see pages 38 and 71–2, for example).

Books to Read. A mixed bag of books suitable for pupils studying for both the Language and Literature examinations of the G.C.E. 'O' Level and C.S.E. Some of the books in each list relate to the passage in Part I of the Unit; others are deliberately varied to cater for wide tastes. These book titles, with others, are arranged according to subject matter on pages 193–7 so that a liking for a particular kind of book or a particular author can be encouraged.

Additional Exercises.

These include interpretation of statistics, a description of a route to follow on a map, and reports on an accident. After these exercises follow sections on:

1. *Prose*, including a list of books arranged according to subject matter. There are hints on how to write about books, fiction and non-fiction, that have been read.

2. *Poetry*, including a list of anthologies useful for most examinations and general reading. Suggestions are made about what to look for in a poem and how to organize answers. A list of topics dealt with in poems is included.

3. *Drama*, which includes a list in alphabetical order according to author of suitable plays.

4. *Oral Work*, which includes a list of subjects used by candidates in their talks which form part of the C.S.E. examination of certain Boards.

The answers to the multiple choice questions are on page 199, which the teacher can remove if he wishes.

Unit 1

I. Reading and Understanding

Read the following passage (which for your convenience has been divided into two sections) and then answer the questions.

THE HISTORY OF HORSE BRASSES

[A]   Lost in the twilight of history are the days when man began to give up hunting and secure part of his living from the land. The first farmers created the first civilizations. Man's efforts alone were not sufficient to till the soil. However advanced his civilization became he could not throw off the ever-present elements. 5
They surrounded him and they alone determined whether or not the harvest was a fruitful one. The forces of good and evil were wrapped in mystery. At a very early time in man's development he became aware of the power of the sun. In a world which seemed hostile it was essential to be able to appease the forces of good and 10
bad, which seemed to be able to send the good or bad weather, and would help or hinder the oxen that pulled the ploughs.

A feature in all primitive societies even today is the acceptance of the idea of the evil eye. This is something which is common throughout the world. It goes back to the roots of all civilization 15
and to this notion we owe the many and varied charms which man has devised in order to avert catastrophe. The horse, and also in earlier days the ox, which pulled the plough was for thousands of years a very important source of power and needed all possible protection against the evil eye. 20

Far away beyond the distant Caspian Sea in Turkmenskaya archaeologists have unearthed amulets left behind by some of the world's earliest farmers in the fifth millennium B.C. Among these we find simple discs marked unmistakably with sunlike rays. There are no written records to tell us how these early agricul- 25
turists used their amulets. It is a fair guess that they would have been very much aware of the sun's power and could have used such charms to protect their livestock.

Much nearer home, from the cairn at Dyffryn Ardudwy in Merionethshire, polished stone pendants have been discovered 30
which doubtless served as amulets. We cannot be sure that people used these charms to protect their livestock but the strong proba-

bility remains. Even in this century farmers in Cumberland used stones with natural holes formed in them which they hung around cows' necks or on the byre door.   35

One of the most interesting English finds dates from Roman times. The bronze bull's head found at Wilcote (Oxfordshire) clearly shows us that the animal had a roundel on its forehead. In Roman days the oxen pulled the plough and we can be reasonably certain that the use of this type of amulet dates at least from this   40 period.

The Celtic era which followed provides us with what may be one of the earliest existing 'brasses'. This was illustrated in the catalogue of the National Museum of Scotland (1892) and shows a leaf-shaped silver plate bearing a sun wheel at its apex. A num-   45 ber of other delicate and probably significant patterns also appear. These include two whorl patterns formed into triskele* designs. We often see these represented as three conjoined legs— an emblem used by the Manxmen. Its origin lies within the sun wheel design and it appears in Scandinavian decoration of the ear-   50 lier Bronze Age, and upon the shields of Greek warriors. We can see therefore just how widespread its use really was.

The fact that a horse's head is also shown on this particular plate also helps to persuade us that it was a horse charm. This silver specimen would have belonged to a chieftain or nobleman.   55 Another find from the Celtic period shows that even warriors used the triskele on their shields. We can appreciate how the emblem became used as a charm to protect man's domestic animals.

[B]   One of the difficulties in tracing the usage of amulets is the lack of any supporting documentary evidence. They came into being long before written history began and as they were objects tinged with superstition they never received any attention from the clerical historians of the Dark Ages. Until early medieval   5 times there is nothing to be gleaned from written records. Illuminated manuscripts do give us a few slender clues about the types of implement used in distant days; but such things were no more than small embellishments to a page border, and very little detail has survived. The quality of the draughtsmanship in those times   10 was very uneven and to the smallness of the pictures we can add the limitations imposed by the artists' skill.

The age of chivalry adds a little to our knowledge. The rich caparisons of the horses used in the joust and on the battlefield show that in addition to various forms of armour the war horse   15 was decorated with plumes that had no functional purpose at all.

---

* a figure consisting of three radiating curves or legs.

The plumes on the horse drawing the brewer's dray seem to be a survival from jousting days, and the relationship becomes stronger when we remember the Shire Horse's ancestors.

It should not be forgotten that folklore provides a strong bond   20
with the remote past and we cannot underrate its importance when considering the form the horse brass took up to the last century. Eighteenth-century brasses do not seem to have survived and perhaps they all found their way into the melting pot in Victoria's reign. The power of very old ideas is still discernible in the   25
countryside and a century ago it was even stronger. In Norfolk, back in 1859, an instance is recorded of a ploughman who always had tied around the neck of his horse the thumb of an old leather glove. When this was stolen by mischievous boys it was found to contain a transcript of the Lord's Prayer. The ploughman claimed   30
that this was an effective charm against the evil eye—one which preserved the horse from all manner of ills including stumbling. This kind of charm is on a parallel with the practice of the Pharisees. In Biblical times they placed a text of scripture in a small box on their foreheads, and it was a common custom for Jewish people   35
to place a text on the lintel of their door.

No one has proved the continuity of the use of an amulet on horses or cattle; so little documentary evidence is to be found. If old traditions did not endure how can we explain so many of the ancient symbols on horse brasses? It is difficult to accept that the   40
Victorian brass designers revived them of their own volition from a past that had not been recorded.

JOHN VINCE, Discovering Horse Brasses (Shire Publications)

MULTIPLE CHOICE QUESTIONS

After reading each of the following questions, choose the ONE correct answer, and indicate it by writing down the letter that stands for it.

From Section A

  1 To speak of the 'twilight of history' (l. 1) is to stress how

    A little we know about the remote past
    B grey and colourless was the life of primitive man
    C gradual were the stages by which man gave up hunting
    D inevitable was the progress that made man a farmer
    E small were man's steps towards achieving civilization

  2 The first paragraph (ll. 1–12) stresses that the progress of early civilizations was

    A difficult

   B rapid
   C puzzling
   D gradual
   E co-operative

3 The idea of 'the evil eye' (l. 14) is that
   A charms to be effective should be in the shape of an eye
   B the essential power of a useful animal lives in its eye
   C all vitality and life is connected with light
   D no-one can avoid bad luck if he is born under the wrong star
   E someone with magical powers can look at a man or animal and ruin his health

4 'Common' (l. 14) means
   A harmful to all who believe it
   B shared by many peoples at many times
   C a reminder of man's irrationality
   D similarly felt by both rich and poor
   E connected with property belonging to the tribe, and not to an individual

5 In line 14 which ONE of the following methods of punctuation would *not* be acceptable?
   A the evil eye—this is something
   B the evil eye, this is something
   C the evil eye: this is something
   D the evil eye; this is something
   E the evil eye! This is something

6 Which ONE of the following phrases is to be taken literally (as opposed to figuratively)? See Part III, Style and Appreciation (6).
   A 'lost in the twilight of history' (l. 1)
   B 'man's efforts alone were not sufficient to till the soil' (ll. 3–4)
   C 'he could not throw off the ever-present elements' (l. 15)
   D 'the forces of good and evil were wrapped in mystery' (ll. 7–8)
   E 'it goes back to the roots of all civilization' (l. 15)

7 The writer leaves vague the meaning of 'catastrophe' (l. 17). He most probably means
   A a failure of the crops due to disease
   B the damage done by an earthquake
   C an eclipse of the sun or moon
   D the death of a valuable draught-animal
   E the damage done by war with another tribe

8 'Amulets' (l. 22) are things worn to
   A prevent a person or an animal from being attacked by evil magic

B symbolize the beauty of a goddess
C complete a horse's harness
D help farmers to identify individual animals
E indicate ownership of a horse

9 All the following words or phrases indicate that the writer is not completely certain of his statements with the ONE EXCEPTION of

A 'lost in the twilight of history' (l. 1)
B 'a feature in all primitive societies . . . is the acceptance of the idea of the evil eye' (ll. 13–14)
C 'There are no written records to tell how these early agriculturists used their amulets' (ll. 25–6)
D 'It is a fair guess that they would have been very much aware of the sun's power' (ll. 26–7)
E 'We cannot be sure that people used these charms to protect their livestock' (ll. 31–2)

10 When writing about primitive people the writer

A regards their superstitions as natural
B stresses how difficult their life was
C regrets the inadequacy of their farming methods
D shows how different they were from the Romans
E despises their beliefs in the evil eye

11 This writer chooses examples from prehistoric central Asia, prehistoric Wales, Roman England, and recent Cumberland to stress that

A man's agricultural technique has improved throughout the ages
B the charms used by different peoples have been very different
C much has been added to our knowledge of this subject by archaeology
D geographical factors have given different peoples different histories
E different people's attempts to protect draught-animals have been very similar

12 Section A is chiefly about how

A superstitions concerning horses have gradually declined
B different religions have had different attitudes to horses
C horse brasses evolved from primitive charms
D using horses as mounts was replaced by using them to pull ploughs
E in all civilizations horses have usually belonged to the rich

13 Section A suggests that man is more than anything else

A inventive
B fond of animals
C religious
D superstitious
E artistic

14 All the following statements about Section A are true EXCEPT that

    A it follows chronological order, progressing from prehistoric times to a period about A.D. 600

    B it deliberately chooses examples from different parts of the world

    C it is interested in the stages by which cavalry become decisive in war

    D it stresses the similarities between the superstitions of different peoples

    E it chooses most of its archaeological examples from the British Isles

From Section B

15 'Documentary evidence' (l. 2) is evidence in

    A legal contracts

    B charters or acts of parliament

    C writing

    D books

    E pictures

16 The priests who wrote history during the Dark Ages (about A.D. 500–1000) ignored amulets because they

    A had not been able to collect any information about them

    B linked them with superstitions that were un-Christian

    C could find no mention of amulets in previous writings

    D used pictures of amulets only as trivial decorations

    E realised that amulets showed a poor level of craftsmanship

17 The author suggests, but does not state, that the ornamental harness worn by horses in medieval tournaments (ll. 13–16)

    A was a deliberate attempt to be less superstitious in equipping horses

    B provides an example of how rich nobles wasted their money on luxuries

    C was an unconscious survival of charms worn by horses in earlier times

    D was completely unconnected with the ways in which Victorians later decorated their horses

    E satisfied military purposes that are now forgotten

18 That 'folklore provides a strong bond with the remote past' (ll. 20–21) means that stories handed down verbally from father to son

    A pass on inaccurate ideas about the remote past that are often misleading

    B keep later generations enslaved to ideas inherited from the past

    C are more valuable than the writings of historians

    D often pass on accurate information about the remote past

    E are ridiculous superstitions, frequently treated as important by ignorant country people

19 'Discernible' (l. 25) means

   A believed by many people
   B gradually declining
   C natural and inevitable
   D easy to trace
   E connected with magic

20 Which ONE of the following words is *not* a metaphor but is used literally? See Part III, Style and Appreciation, (6).

   A 'tinged' (l. 4)
   B 'gleaned' (l. 6)
   C 'quality' (l. 10)
   D 'bond' (l. 20)
   E 'on a parallel with' (l. 33)

21 The important point about the Norfolk ploughman (ll. 26–32) was that he

   A was so superstitious that he almost invited mischievous boys to tease him
   B was very different from farm workers today
   C was using what was really a magical charm
   D was putting a Bible text to an irreligious use
   E had not been educated at all

22 The 'continuity of the use of an amulet on horses' (l. 37) is

   A proved by the evidence produced by this writer
   B more probable in some areas than in others
   C disputed by some writers and believed by others
   D an idea that is relevant to only some of the examples included in Sections A and B
   E believed by this author though it cannot be proved

23 Which ONE of the following ideas would you omit if you were summarizing the main points of Section B?

   A little has been written about amulets, though monks included illustrations of them in manuscripts
   B medieval knights had plumes on their horses and this tradition was perhaps passed on to carthorses in later times
   C the opinions of common people about superstition were often handed down by word of mouth
   D connection between past superstitions and modern horse brasses probably existed, though they cannot be proved
   E Victorian designers of horse brasses re-invented them

TRADITIONAL QUESTIONS

Answer the following questions in your own words as far as possible. Questions marked with an asterisk should be answered *very briefly*, and in these answers complete sentences are not necessary.

From Section A

*1 Give in a single word or short phrase the meaning of *five* of the following words *as used in the passage*:

i appease (l. 10)   ii devised (l. 17)   iii cairn (l. 29)   iv byre (l. 35)
v whorl (l. 47)   vi plate (l. 54)

2 What does the metaphor 'wrapped in mystery' (l. 8) convey that a plain statement would lack? See Part III, Using English, (6).

3 What do you think is meant by the expression 'the evil eye' (l. 14)?

4 'Man's efforts alone were not sufficient to till the soil' (ll. 3–4). What steps did men take to become successful farmers?

5 Show the steps by which the author proceeds from man the hunter to the main subject of the passage, horse brasses.

6 What is the connection between the sun and horse brasses, according to the author?

From Section B

*7 Give in a single word or short phrase the meaning of *four* of the following words *as used in the passage*:

i implement (l. 8)   ii embellishments (l. 9)   iii functional (l. 16)
iv transcript (l. 30)   v volition (l. 41)

8 Why is it difficult to trace the history of the use of amulets?

9 Why did not the historians of the Dark Ages mention amulets?

10 What is meant by 'illuminated manuscripts' (ll. 6–7)?

11 Comment on the use of the following words:
i 'tinged' (l. 4)   ii 'gleaned' (l. 6)   iii 'parallel' (l. 33)

12 What is the meaning of the following expressions:
i 'give us a few slender clues' (l. 7)   ii 'provides a strong bond with' (ll. 20–21)?

13 Why does the writer introduce the subject of folk-lore, and what connection has it with horse brasses?

From the whole passage

14 Why does the writer think that Victorian horse brasses are a continuation of the use of charms for the protection of horses by primitive man?

II. Writing English

Write on ONE of the following:

a Show how superstition affects the lives of many people today. Illustrate your answer with short stories confirming your views. The stories you use may be real or invented.

b Horse power.

c Assume that our sources of energy—coal, oil etc.—will be exhausted by the year A.D. 2000. Picture life as you think it will be in this country and in particular in your own locality.

d Are we wasting time and money in extending our road system?

e Write a story describing your adventures on a canoeing holiday or a pony-trekking holiday. Introduce people whom you meet into your story, and describe the places you visit, trying to give the reader atmosphere as well as incident.

f 'Made redundant.' (You may treat this as a story or a discussion.)

g What point is there in exploring space?

h Write a vivid description of two of the following:

   i A fish and chip shop at lunchtime on Saturday
   ii A football ground after a goal has been scored
  iii Your family watching a particular television programme
  iv A crowded beach on a sunny Bank Holiday

i Write a story, a description or an essay suggested by the illustration above. (Your composition may be directly about the subject of the illustration, or may only take suggestions from it, but there must be some clear connection between the illustration and the composition.)

Suggestions for Projects, Assignments and Course Work

1 Books through the Ages: ancient Egypt and China—scrolls— monasteries and manuscripts—printing—paper—paperbacks. Use your school or local library reference books for subject matter.

2 Science fiction: branches of science—time, space, abnormal vege- tation or animal life—early writings—recent developments. Read books by H. G. Wells, Arthur C. Clarke, Ray Bradbury, Brian Aldiss. (See pages 192–3.)

III. Using English

Punctuation

Revise uses of full stop (end of sentences; abbreviations) and comma (lists; sentence adverb as in 'However, ...'; nominative of address as in 'John, come here.') Include capital letters in the revision of the full stop.

Sometimes 'revision' includes work which has not been understood in previous lessons. Punctuation can be improved by the dictation of suit- able short passages. At first the pauses required by full stops and commas may be over-emphasized in the reading. This sometimes leads to a better understanding of the need for punctuation. For abler pupils the deliber- ate ignoring of punctuation in a dictated passage, and the consequent misphrasing, provide the lighter side of punctuation practice.

   1 Account for the following marks of punctuation in the passage in Part I:
   i the semi-colon after 'days' (l.B. 8)   **ii** the semi-colon after 'cattle' (l.B. 38)   **iii** the brackets before and after 'Oxfordshire' (l.A. 37) **iv** the dash after 'legs' (l.A. 48)   **v** the dash after 'eye' (l.B. 31).

Grammar and Usage

Revision of parts of speech, especially noun, pronoun and adjective. Any necessary revision of Number, Person and Gender.

2 Write sentences using the following as different parts of speech: place (noun and verb); by (preposition and adverb); over (noun, preposi- tion and adverb); weekly (adjective and adverb).

3 The following words describe water in motion: jet, splash, shower, stream. Write down as many words as you can which describe air in motion.

Spelling and Dictionary Work

Make sure you know the meaning of the symbols used to give infor- mation about the words in your dictionary.

4 Find the following words and write down their etymology—this word is also in the dictionary!

i anecdote ii amulet iii emblem iv superstition v caparison vi joust vii volition.

5 'ie' and 'ei'. Revise the 'i' before 'e' rule. In words with the 'ee' sound, 'i' before 'e' except after 'c'.

As usual in English spelling, there are exceptions to the rule, the most common being: seize, weird, weir, counterfeit, protein, plebeian.

Try these: rec . . ve, bes . . ge, bel . . ve, gr . . ved, rel . . f, dec . . ve.

Style and Appreciation

6 Understanding and explaining simile and metaphor.

'His thirst for knowledge is unquenchable!' This sentence uses the words 'thirst' and 'unquenchable' in connection with 'knowledge'. In this sentence 'knowledge' is used literally, but 'thirst' and 'unquenchable', because they do not refer to an actual physical thirst, are metaphorical. The connection of these two very different ideas is explained by using an 'equation'. Put the literal word(s) on one side of an = sign and the metaphorical on the other side:

$$\text{thirst unquenchable} = \text{knowledge}$$

The two sides must now be made equal, and this will produce a literal expression on both sides of the equation:

a thirst which cannot be quenched by drinking = (is like)
a desire for knowledge which cannot be fulfilled

Perhaps the explanation could be put the other way:

A desire for knowledge which cannot be fulfilled is like a thirst which cannot be satisfied by drinking.

All metaphors, like similes, contain comparisons between objects which at first sight appear to be unlike or even opposite in character. Similes should be dealt with by the same method. H. E. Bates used the following description of water-lily leaves on a pond. 'The olive-yellow lily-pads in high summer covered every inch of water like plates of emerald porcelain.'

Follow the procedure outlined above:

olive-yellow lily-pads = (are like) plates of emerald porcelain.

Do not confine yourself to the sense of sight. There may be likenesses which can be perceived by the senses of hearing, taste, touch or smell.

Flat leaves (pads) = flat plates; colour; texture. A final version might read:

Olive-yellow lily-pads are compared with plates of emerald

porcelain because both are flat, of the same colour and are alike in texture.

Size and shape might be included.

This is what is required when you are asked to 'explain', 'comment on' etc, figures of speech. Such a procedure shows that you have understood the underlying likeness.

Try to explain the meaning, using the same method, of 'twilight of history' (l.A. 1) in Part I.

Books to read

The following books, varied in content and style, should provide the sort of reading necessary for CSE Literature papers and general background information for composition work in the Language papers of GCE 'O' Level and the CSE.

For poetry and drama, see pages 191, 192, 196 and 197.

Brave New World	Aldous Huxley
1984	George Orwell
Lord of the Flies	William Golding
Lorna Doone	R. D. Blackmore
The Cry of a Bird	Dorothy Yglesias
The Road to Wigan Pier	George Orwell
One, Two, Buckle my Shoe	Agatha Christie
One of our Submarines	Edward Young
Short Stories	Muriel Spark
Four Tales	Joseph Conrad

Unit 2

I. Reading and Understanding

In two of his books about collecting wild animals, Gerald Durrell describes Mamfe, a town in the Cameroons (West Africa), which was ruled by Britain until it obtained its independence in the 1960s. Here are parts of his two descriptions. Section C is part of the first description; Section A and B are part of the second.

Read the following passage (which for your convenience has been divided into three sections) and then answer the questions.

TWO VIEWS OF MAMFE IN WEST AFRICA

[A]   Mamfe is not the most salubrious of places, perched as it is on a promontory above the curve of a great, brown river and surrounded by dense rain forest. It is as hot and moist as a Turkish bath for most of the year, only deviating from this monotony during the rainy season when it becomes hotter and moister.   5

At that time it had a resident population of five white men, one white woman, and some ten thousand vociferous Africans. I, in a moment of mental aberration, had made this my headquarters for an animal collection expedition and was occupying a large marquee full of assorted wild animals on the banks of the brown,   10
hippo-reverberating river. In the course of my work I had, of course, come to know the white population. The Africans acted as my hunters, guides and carriers, for when you went into that forest you were transported back into the days of Stanley and Livingstone and all your worldly possessions had to be carried on   15
the heads of a line of stalwart carriers.

Collecting wild animals is a full-time occupation and one does not have much time for the social graces, but it was curiously enough in this unlikely spot that I had the opportunity of helping what was then known as the Colonial Office.   20

I was busy one morning with the task of giving milk to five unweaned baby squirrels, none of whom, it appeared, had any brain or desire to live. At that time no feeding bottle with a small enough teat to fit the minute mouth of a baby squirrel had been invented, so the process was that you wrapped cotton wool round the end of   25
a matchstick, dipped it into the milk mixture, and put it into their mouths for them to suck. This was a prolonged and extremely irri-

tating job, for you had to be careful not to put too much milk on
the cotton wool, otherwise they would choke, and you had to slip
the cotton wool into their mouths sideways, otherwise it would   30
catch on their teeth, whereupon they would promptly swallow it
and die of an impacted bowel.

It was ten o'clock in the morning and already the heat was so intense that I had to keep wiping my hands on a towel so that I did
not drench the baby squirrels with my sweat and thus give them a   35
chill. I was not in the best of tempers but while I was trying to get
some sustenance into my protégés (who were not collaborating),
my steward, Pious, suddenly materialized at my side in the silent,
unnerving way that Africans have.

'Please, sah,' he said.   40

'Yes, whatee?' I inquired irritably, trying to push some milk-
drenched cotton wool into a squirrel's mouth.

'D.O. come, sah,' he said.

'The District Officer?' I asked in astonishment. 'What the hell
does he want?'   45

'No say, sah,' said Pious impassively. 'I go open beer?'

'Well, I suppose you'd better,' I said, and as Martin Bugler, the
District Officer, arrived at the crest of the hill I pushed the squirrels back into their nestbox full of dried banana leaves and went
out of the marquee to greet him.   50

[B]   Martin was a tall, gangling young man with round, almost-
black eyes and floppy black hair, a snub nose and a wide and very
ingratiating grin. Owing to the length of his arms and legs and his
habit of making wild gestures to illustrate when he talked, he was
accident prone. But he was, however, a remarkably good D.O. for   5
he loved his job intensely and, what is even more important, he
loved the Africans equally intensely and they responded to this.

Now it has become fashionable to run down colonialism, District Officers and their assistants are made out to be monsters of
iniquity. Of course there were bad ones but the majority of them   10
were a wonderful set of men who did an exceedingly difficult job
under the most trying conditions. Imagine, at the age of twenty-
eight being put in charge of an area, say, the size of Wales, popu-
lated by an enormous number of Africans and with one assistant
to help you. You had to look after their every need, you had to be   15
mother and father to them, and you had to dispense the law. And
in many cases the law, being English law, was of such complexity
that it defeated even the devious brain of the indigenous population.

On many occasions, on my forays into the forest, I had passed   20

the big mud-brick courtroom with its tin roof and seen Martin—
the sweat pouring down him in torrents—trying some case or
other, the whole thing being made even more complicated by the
fact that villages, sometimes separated only by a few miles, spoke
different dialects. Therefore, should there be dissension between   25
two villages, it meant that you had to have two interpreters from
the two villages, and an interpreter who knew both dialects who
could then interpret Martin. As in courts of law anywhere in the
world, you knew perfectly well that everybody was lying the hind
leg off a donkey, I had the greatest admiration for Martin's   30
patience and solemnity on these occasions. The cases could range
from suspected cannibalism, via wife stealing, to simple things
like whose cocoa-yam patch was invading whose, inch by subtle
inch.

I was very surprised at Martin's appearance because, at that   35
time in the morning, he should have been up to his eyes in office
work. He came down the hillside almost at a run, gesticulating like
a windmill and shouting things at me that I could not hear.

GERALD DURRELL, *Fillets of Plaice* (Collins).

[C]   The Cross River picks its way down from the mountains of
the Cameroons, until it runs sprawling and glittering into the
great bowl of forest land around Mamfe. After being all froth,
waterfalls and eager chattering in the mountains, it settles down
when it reaches this forest, and runs sedately in its rocky bed, the   5
gently moving waters creating ribs of pure white sand across its
width, and washing the mud away from the tree roots, so that they
look as though they stand at the edge of the water on a tangled,
writhing mass of octopus-like legs. It moves along majestically, its
brown waters full of hippo and crocodile, and the warm air above   10
it filled with hawking swallows, blue and orange and white.

Just above Mamfe the river increases its pace slightly, squeezing
itself between two high rocky cliffs, cliffs that are worn smooth by
the passing waters and wear a tattered antimacassar of undergrowth that hangs down from the forest above; emerging from the   15
gorge it swirls out into a vast egg-shaped basin. A little further
along, through an identical gorge, another river empties itself into
this same basin, and the waters meet and mix in a skein of tiny currents, whirlpools and ripples, and then continue onwards as one
waterway, leaving, as a result of their marriage, a huge glittering   20
hummock of white sand in the centre of the river, sand that is
pockmarked with the footprints of hippo and patterned with
chains of bird-tracks. Near this island of sand the forest on the
bank gives way to the small grassfield that surrounds the village of

Mamfe, and it was here, on the edge of the forest, above the   25
smooth brown river, that we chose to have our base camp.

It took two days of cutting and levelling to get the camp site
ready, and on the third day Smith and I stood at the edge of the
grassfield watching while thirty sweating, shouting Africans
hauled and pulled at what appeared to be the vast, brown,   30
wrinkled carcase of a whale that lay on the freshly turned red
earth. Gradually, as this sea of canvas was pulled and pushed, it
rose into the air, swelling like an unhealthy looking puffball. Then
it seemed to spread out suddenly, leech-like, and turned itself into
a marquee of impressive dimensions. When it had thus revealed its   35
identity, there came a full-throated roar, a mixture of astonishment, amazement and delight, from the crowd of villagers who
had come to watch our camp building.

Once the marquee was ready to house us, it took another week
of hard work before we were ready to start collecting. Cages had   40
to be erected, ponds dug, various chiefs from nearby villages inter-
viewed and told of the animals we required, food supplies had to
be laid on, and a hundred and one other things had to be done.
Eventually, when the camp was functioning smoothly, we felt we
could start collecting in earnest. We had decided that Smith   45
should stay in Mamfe and keep the base camp going, gleaning
what forest fauna he could with the help of the local inhabitants,
while I was to travel further inland to the mountains, where the
forest gave place to the great grasslands. In this mountain world,
with its strange vegetation and cooler climate, a completely differ-   50
ent fauna from that of the steamy forest region was to be found.

I was not certain which part of the grasslands would be the best
for me to operate in, so I went to the District Officer for advice. I
explained my dilemma, and he produced a map of the mountains
and together we pored over it.   55

GERALD DURRELL, *The Bafut Beagles* (Rupert Hart-Davis)

MULTIPLE CHOICE QUESTIONS

After reading each of the following questions, choose the ONE correct
answer, and indicate it by writing down the letter that stands for it.

From Section A

1 'Salubrious' (l. 1) means
   A healthy
   B wholesome
   C sanitary
   D prosperous
   E attractive

2 'Vociferous' (l. 7) means

  A excited
  B rebellious
  C noisy
  D hungry
  E laughing

3 By using words such as 'not salubrious' (l. 1) and 'aberration' (l. 8) Durrell suggests that as a site for his headquarters Mamfe was

  A too remote from the animals' homes
  B surprisingly disappointing
  C slightly inconvenient
  D very unsuitable
  E forced on him by circumstances

4 If you were summarizing the main ideas of ll. 21–39 which ONE of the following would you *not* include?

  A the baby squirrels were co-operating with Durrell's efforts because of their strong will to live
  B Durrell got them to suck at some cotton wool soaked in milk and wrapped round a matchstick
  C Durrell had to avoid putting too much milk on the cotton wool, since this would cause the young squirrels to choke
  D if Durrell failed to insert the cotton wool sideways then the squirrels would swallow it and injure their internal organs
  E there was the danger that Durrell's perspiration would given the squirrels a chill

5 When Durrell says 'Well, I suppose you'd better' (l. 47) he speaks with

  A an obvious irritation
  B a complete change of mood
  C a resolve to be polite
  D a sense of anxiety
  E a grudging consent

From Section B

6 Martin's 'grin' (l. 3)

  A was a compliment to his listener
  B prevented one from taking him seriously
  C showed that he knew he had made a mistake
  D made him likable
  E proved that he did not take life seriously

7 Durrell believes that District Officers were

  A often very evil
  B usually conscientious
  C too young for their responsibilities

    D unconsciously fond of power

    E attempting an impossible task

8 Which ONE of the following points does Durrell *not* make in discussing law suits in Mamfe?

    A the laws that had to be enforced were very complicated

    B people from different villages spoke different dialects

    C most witnesses in most cases told lies

    D the cases tried varied very much in their nature and their seriousness

    E the best solution was to concentrate quickly on essentials

9 'Indigenous' (l. 18) means

    A not provided with adequate food

    B born in the province

    C incapable of reading and writing

    D too eager to go to law

    E without their essential freedom

10 There is an element of irony (saying the opposite of what he means) in Durrell's use of the word

    A 'wild' (l. 4)

    B 'good' (l. 5)

    C 'intensely (l. 6)

    D 'colonialism' (l. 8)

    E 'simple' (l. 32)

11 'Gesticulating' (l. 37) means

    A raising an alarm

    B waving his arms about

    C plainly showing his feelings

    D attracting attention

    E acting a sort of pantomime

12 Which ONE of the following remarks does *not* convey a slight suggestion of humour?

    A 'Now it has become fashionable to run down colonialism' (l. 8)

    B 'you knew perfectly well that everybody was lying the hind leg off a donkey' (ll. 29–30)

    C 'The cases could range from suspected cannibalism, via wife stealing, to . . . .' (ll. 31–2)

    D simple things like whose cocoa-yam patch was invading whose' (ll. 32–3)

    E 'gesticulating like a windmill' (ll. 37–8)

13 Which ONE of the following comments about punctuation is *not* true?

    A the parenthesis *what is even more important* (l. 6) might very correctly have had two dashes instead of two commas

B the comma after *colonialism* (l. 8) shows that the preceding clause tells us when the action of the main sentence occurs, and could very well have begun 'Now that it . . .'

C the commas in ll. 15–16 separate the three essential facts about a good District Officer

D the commas in l. 20 show that the phrase *on my forays into the forest* is completely essential to the sense of the passage

E the comma after *whose* (l. 33) puts a certain amount of emphasis on the last four words

From Section C

14 Which ONE of the following words does *not* treat the Cross River as a human person?

A 'picks' (its way) (l. 1)

B 'sprawling' (l. 2)

C 'glittering' (l. 2)

D 'chattering' (l. 4)

E 'squeezing' (itself) (l. 12)

15 Which ONE of the following remarks about the punctuation is *not* correct?

A the comma after *Cameroons* (l. 2) is not completely essential, because the words that follow it tell us for how long the Cross River 'picks its way down from the mountains'

B in ll. 3–4 there is a list of three nouns; a comma divides the first from the second, and the word *and* divides the second from the third

C the semi-colon in l. 15 separates the descriptions of two different reaches of the river—entering the gorge and leaving it

D the commas in l. 13 (after *cliffs*) and l. 26 (after *river*) are similar; both introduce a phrase that partly repeats and partly expands what has gone before

E the comma after *going* in l. 46 divides the sentence into two halves, each dealing with a different type of animal-collecting

16 The comma after *river* in l. 26 could quite well have been replaced by a

A dash

B colon

C semi-colon

D full stop

E exclamation mark

17 Which ONE of the following remarks about comparisons is *not* true?

A the word 'hawking' (l. 11) describes how the swallows dive steeply downwards

B ll. 15–16 explain that after leaving the gorge the river enters an oval-shaped river valley

C l. 18 describes how the waters of two rivers merge into one stream just as strands of woollen yarn unite into one coil or *skein*

D In l. 20 the union of two rivers is compared to the wedding of a man and woman

    E In l. 32 the canvas of a completed marquee rising in the air is compared to a wave of the sea throwing itself upwards towards the shore

18 Which ONE of the following would you omit if you were describing the main sections of the Cross River?

    A it descends tumultuously, by means of many waterfalls, down the mountain-sides

    B it becomes a quieter, steadier stream when it reaches the equatorial forests

    C it runs rather faster through a narrow gorge till it has a turbulent meeting with a similar river

    D at this point it produces many parallel sand bars and piles up mud against the trees

    E the combined rivers unite to form one large, powerful stream near Mamfe

19 The word 'gleaning' (l. 46) suggests that, compared with the animals collected by Durrell himself, those collected by Smith would be

    A more varied in species

    B of greater variety

    C fewer in number

    D of less value

    E more numerous in autumn

From the whole Passage

20 If we contrast the style of Section C with that of the other Sections it appears

    A less formal

    B less literary

    C more personal

    D more metaphorical

    E more complimentary

21 Section C (in contrast to A and B) says less about

    A the differences between the various stretches of the Cross River

    B the visual appearance of Mamfe and its surroundings

    C the difficulties of collecting animals in a hot climate

    D the enthusiasm of Durrell's native helpers

    E Durrell's plans for collecting wild animals

22 Which ONE of the following is *not* true about Sections A and B, as distinct from C?

    A they deal with an occasion when the District Officer visits Durrell, rather than the other way round

    B they say more about Durrell's bad temper

    C they stress the conscientiousness of most white officials when Britain still ruled parts of Africa

  D they have fewer words such as *majestically* or *glittering* that make West Africa seem picturesque
  E they say less about keeping animals alive after capture than about planning to catch them

TRADITIONAL QUESTIONS

Answer the following questions in your own words as far as possible. Questions marked with an asterisk should be answered *very briefly*, and in these answers complete sentences are not necessary.

From Section A

  *1 Give in a single word or short phrase the meaning of *five* of the following words *as used in the passage*:
  i salubrious (l.1) **ii** promontory (l.2) **iii** vociferous (l.7)
  iv stalwart (l.16) **v** sustenance (l.37) **vi** protégés (l.37)
  vii impassively (l.46)

  2 What does the figurative expression 'perched' (l.1) convey that a plain statement would lack? (See Part III of Unit I.)

  3 Explain the meaning of the following:
  i 'mental aberration' (l.8) **ii** 'hippo-reverberating' (l.11)
  iii 'social graces' (l.18)

  4 In about forty of your own words summarize the difficulties of feeding the baby squirrels.

  5 Pick out and comment on one simile. (See Part III of Unit I.)

  *6 Suggest a word to describe the mood of the writer on the morning described in this section.

  7 Choose one phrase or sentence that includes an element of humour, and justify your choice.

From Section B

  *8 Give in a single word or short phrase the meaning of *four* of the following words *as used in the passage*:
  i gangling (l.1) **ii** ingratiating (l.3) **iii** iniquity (l.10)
  iv indigenous (l.18) **v** forays (l.20) **vi** dissension (l.25)

  9 Explain the following expressions:
  i 'accident prone' (l.5) **ii** 'gesticulating like a windmill' (l.37)

  10 In about 50 words summarize the difficulties of a District Officer as described in Section B.

*11 Quote *two* expressions from this section to show that Durrell admires the District Officer.

From Section C

*12 Give in a single word or short phrase the meaning of *five* of the following *as used in the passage*:
   i sedately (l. 5)   **ii** hummock (l. 21)   **iii** full-throated (l. 36)
   iv fauna (l. 47)   **v** dilemma (l. 54)   **vi** pored over (l. 55)

13 Explain the comparison in each of the following metaphors (See Unit I, Part III, Style and Appreciation):
   i bowl (l. 3)   **ii** ribs (l. 6)   **iii** hawking (l. 11)   **iv** marriage (l. 20)
   v pockmarked (l. 22)   **vi** gleaning (l. 46)

14 Explain the expression 'a tattered antimacassar of undergrowth' (ll. 14–15). Is it completely appropriate in this context?

15 Explain the stages in the river's journey to the sea that are suggested by each of the following phrases:
   i 'picks its way' (l. 1)   **ii** 'sprawling and glittering' (l. 2)   **iii** 'eager chattering' (l. 4)   **iv** 'moves along majestically' (l. 9)   **v** 'increases its pace' (l.12)   **vi** 'squeezing itself' (ll.12–13)   **vii** 'it swirls out' (l.16)   **vii** 'empties itself' (l.17)

From the Whole Passage

16 What do you learn about Martin Bugler from Sections A and B?

17 What do Sections A and B say about the difficulties of collecting animals in Africa that Section C omits?

18 What other differences of subject matter or emphasis do you notice between the account in A and B and the other account in C?

II. Writing English

Write on ONE of the following:

a An account of an expedition in search of . . . . (supply the object of your search). Include description of scenery and climate in your narrative.
b 'Now it has become fashionable to run down colonialism.' What are your views?
c Unusual pets.
d Odd man out.
e Your favourite science fiction story. Give a brief outline of the plot. Describe the characters, saying whether you find them credible. Say why you prefer this story to other science fiction stories that you have read.

f Write a letter to the Clerk of your local Council asking for improvements in local services, e.g. cheap fares for senior citizens, bus shelters, provision of playing fields, nursery schools, street cleaning and refuse collecting, parking facilities, premises for youth activities etc. Give examples of particular failures in order to support your case.

g Describe a stretch of coastline, an estuary, or a river which has a character of its own. Try to use the methods adopted by the writer in Section C of Part I.

h My ski-ing holiday. Imagine yourself a learner or an experienced performer. Give details of preparations, training, adventures and return home.

Suggested Projects, Assignments and Course Work

1 Write a critical evaluation of books, short stories, films and television programmes that deal with one of the following:

   i a definite local area of the country
   ii the Generation Gap
   iii changing ideas of morality

2 Discuss two biographies that you have read, one of a person whom you admire, and one of a person whom you do not.

3 Write a story about a family who give up their house in a town and go to live in a caravan in the country. Try to imagine some of the problems that might face them, some of the things that might go wrong, and how they would react to them.

4 Suppose a Martian landed secretly in Britain. Imagine that on Mars some things (e.g. bringing up babies) are very similar but other things (e.g. transport, treatment of criminals) are very different. Write the account of this visit that the Martian might contribute to a Martian newspaper on his return to Mars.

III. Using English

Punctuation

Revise uses of the comma (noun or noun phrase in apposition as in 'Tom, the piper's son,'; adverb phrases/clauses, depending on position in sentence; participial phrases as in 'Having no desire to walk, I took a taxi.') N.B. Adjective clauses: see 3 below.
See Unit I, Part III, for suggestions about revision of punctuation.

1 Pick out and account for three different uses of the hyphen from the passage in Part I.

2 Comment on the use of the apostrophe in 'o'clock' (l.A.33) and 'squirrel's' (l.A. 42).

3 A defining adjective clause is necessary to the sense of a sentence and is not separated from the rest of the sentence by commas, for example:

>All the refugees *who needed help* were given food, but the others continued their journey.

A non-defining clause is not necessary to the sense of a sentence and is marked off by commas:

>The refugees, *all of whom came from the Far East*, were given food.

Add **a** a defining adjective clause **b** a non-defining adjective clause to each of the following sentences (a total of six sentences).

   i The month of November was very wet
   ii The Lake District continues to attract more and more visitors
   iii The difference between 'I will' and 'I shall' is ignored by the Americans.

Grammar and Usage

4 Use the following words in separate sentences as different parts of speech: **i** minute **ii** snub **iii** prone **iv** set **v** brand **vi** base.

5 Write out the following expressions making all the nouns plural:
   i the boy's nose **ii** the minstrel's banjo **iii** the printer's proof
   iv the doctor's medicine **v** the zoo's rhinoceros **vi** the index of the book **vii** the princess's diadem.

6 Use prefixes that mean 'not' with the following words to produce words of opposite meaning, e.g. necessary—un-necessary:
   i settled **ii** probable **iii** proper **iv** true **v** population
   vi band (verb) **vii** order **viii** constant.

Spelling and Dictionary Work

7 Revise the y/i rule. Study the following examples:
   a tidy — tidiness; busy — business; victory — victorious; story — stories
   b storey — storeys; enjoy — enjoyment
   c marry — marrying; apply — applying; rely — relying
Note the difference in treatment of 'y' followed by a suffix. Try to think of exceptions to the above 'rules', e.g. say—said.

8 Find out the origins of the following words by using a dictionary
   i canter **ii** laconic **iii** tawdry **iv** navy **v** bungalow
   vi dragoon **vii** vociferous **viii** furtive **ix** chameleon
   x helicopter **xi** tulip **xii** turquoise **xiii** chivalry **xiv** ranch
   xv peninsula **xvi** albatross.

9 Show the difference in use or meaning, by any method you choose, between the words in the following pairs: **i** prophecy, prophesy
   ii advice, advise **iii** principal, principle **iv** lightening, lightning
   v passed, past **vi** dependant, dependent **vii** continual, continuous.

Style and appreciation

10 'The sweat pouring down him in torrents' (l.B. 22) deliberately exaggerates—a figure of speech called hyperbole. We are not meant to take the statement literally. We often exaggerate for emphasis: 'she cried her eyes out' or 'he lost his head'. Write five sentences, each containing an example of hyperbole that you have heard people use or have seen in a book.

11 All three sections of the passage in Part I were written by the same author. Show how the first two sections differ from the third in style and try to account for these differences.

Books to read

King Solomon's Mines	H. Rider Haggard
Walkabout	J.V. Marshall
To Kill a Mockingbird	Harper Lee
Snake Man	Alan Wykes
Bhowani Junction	John Masters
Cry, the Beloved Country	Alan Paton
Typhoon	Joseph Conrad
The Overloaded Ark	Gerald Durrell
A Pattern of Islands	Arthur Grimble
Return to the Islands	Arthur Grimble
Short Stories	Algernon Blackwood
In Hazard	Richard Hughes

Unit 3

I. Reading and Understanding

Read the following passage (which for your convenience has been divided into three sections) and then answer the questions.

TWO FIRMS OF GLOUCESTERSHIRE DEALERS

[A]   It is the job and the livelihood of a dealer to buy cheap and to sell dear; if he fails to do that he goes bankrupt. In order to buy cheap he must either take pains to discredit the article he wants to buy, declaring in the presence of the whole company that it is a fake, its legs are broken, it isn't worth a pound, he bought one like   5
it last week for five bob, et cetera, et cetera, meanwhile arranging with a friend to buy it on his behalf; or alternatively he must arrange with the other dealers present to form a 'ring', i.e. not to bid against each other, and to share out their purchases equally after the sale. Neither practice could be considered ethically   10
sound; but if you are a dealer in anything you can't afford to consider ethics.

However, I suppose by a stretch of imagination you might call these tricks negatively honest rather than positively dishonest. The positive malpractices of the dealers are varied and ingenious.   15

Elmbury had two firms of dealers who carried on business in the town. The one was Smith Brothers, the other Percy Parfitt. Mr Parfitt was a craftsman as well as a crook. The Smith Brothers were altogether different. Albert was tall and flashy, Eric was squat and scruffy-looking. They preyed mainly upon country cot-   20
tages and the inhabitants of the villages. Eric, riding upon a bi-cycle, would make the first reconnaissance, calling at the cottages and inquiring 'whether the missus had any odd bits of furniture to sell'. If he was asked in and allowed to rout round he would delib-erately fix his attention upon something trivial and worthless,   25
declaring 'That's a very nice engraving,' or 'That's a very inter-esting little table—might be worth a lot of money if it's genuine.' Meanwhile he would perhaps discover something, let us say an antique oak chest, which was really valuable; but he would appear to take no notice of it or would dismiss it as being worthless.   30
Instead he would return again and again to the little table, shaking his head over it gravely: 'Wish I knew more about antiques,

Missus, I'm not much better than an old junk merchant myself. But I've got a hunch about this little table. Might be real Queen Anne. Might be worth a tenner. But I couldn't risk a tenner on it   35
myself. Now I've got a friend in London who knows about these things. I do a bit of business with him—just junk, you know—and if ever he's down in these parts I'll bring him along to have a look at that little table of yourn.'

So saying, Mr Eric Smith would depart upon his rickety bicycle.   40
The cottager, being no fool, took the earliest opportunity to find out the real worth of the table; and found out that it was worth about ten bob. Guileless old women are rare in country cottages; and the Smith Brothers and their kind had long ago discovered and fleeced the last of them. Eric and Albert relied now on making   45
their profit not out of the guileless but out of the most cunning: the ones who would take the trouble to get the local connoisseur's opinion on the value of the table and who, finding it worthless, would eagerly await the coming of that mug who was Mr Eric Smith's friend from London.   50

[B]   In due course the friend from London arrived. This was Albert, dressed in fearful plus-fours and driving a respectable motor-car. 'My friend, Mr Smith,' said Albert, 'told me you might let me have a look at your little table . . . . . .'

Having examined it, shaken his head over it, turned it upside   5
down and looked at the worm-holes through a magnifying glass, Albert would inform the delighted cottager that it might—it might just possibly—be genuine Queen Anne; and he'd be prepared to take a risk and offer fifteen pounds for it. The cottager, knowing the thing was worth ten shillings, would promptly accept   10
the offer; and then Albert would count up his money and find that he only had five pounds.

'I could write you a cheque,' he would say doubtfully, 'but I couldn't expect you to trust me, could I, being a stranger?'

The cottager, wise in the ways of crooks from London, would   15
indicate politely that he preferred to receive cash.

'Quite right,' said Albert cheerfully. 'No offence taken, I assure you. But I'll tell you what I'll do. I'll be passing this way to-morrow and I'll bring the cash then. Meanwhile you'll keep the table for me?'   20

That sounded fair and honest enough. Albert shook hands with his victim and prepared to leave; but as he was putting on his coat his glance fell upon that valuable oak chest which brother Eric had told of. He took a casual look at it and said: 'It's not a bad little chest; but there's not much sale for such things to-day. If you   25 like—since I'm buying the table—I'll give you another ten bob and take the chest as well.'

Now the cottager, probably, didn't know the value of the chest; but even if she thought that it was worth two or three pounds, she felt inclined to let it go, in view of the huge price she was getting for   30
the table. Perhaps she haggled a bit, then said:

'Very well, you can have it for a pound.'

'Done,' said Albert, 'and since I've got the cash I'll pay you for the chest straight away. I shan't have room in the car for both chest and table when I call to-morrow.'   35

So Albert went off with the chest, having bought it for a pound, whereas it was worth twenty. 'See you to-morrow,' he called out from the car. 'Don't sell the table to any one else, mind, before I come back!'

But of course he never came back. He never meant to come   40
back. The cottager was left with her worthless table; and it was generally quite a long time before she realized that Mr Smith's friend from London had cheated her out of nineteen pounds.

And when she did realize it, she had no remedy; for Albert hadn't committed any offence for which she could prosecute him.   45
He had simply changed his mind about buying the table; and a chap couldn't be punished for changing his mind.

Forty years in business, said the Smith Brothers, and a tricky business at that; and never broke the law once save when Albert forgot to renew his driving licence and when an interfering bobby   50
copped Eric for bicycling without a light: things that might happen to anybody. Virtuous citizens of Elmsbury were the Smith Brothers, and great respecters of the Law; unlike some people they might name but wouldn't who stooped to practices abomin-able in the eyes of Albert and Eric and all upright men—practices,   55
for example, such as those of Mister P. P. (no names, no packdrill) who had a workshop behind his business premises, and what went on in that workshop, in the way of faking and fiddling and turning modern junk into genuine antiques—well, the Smith Brothers would blush to tell you.   60

[C]   For my part I liked Mr Parfitt a great deal better than I liked the Smiths. I liked him for his merry crinkled smile, for his crafts-man's love of his trade (even though it was a dishonest trade), and for the fact that he never cheated anybody who didn't deserve to be cheated; which was more than you could say of Albert and   5
Eric.

He had a shop in the unfashionable part of the High Street. Over the door hung the simple, austere and untruthful sign,

'ANTIQUES'. You went into a small low room which was always
very dark (it was necessary that it should be dark) and out of the   10
shadows, himself like a Shade, there came shuffling towards you
the small, wizened form of Mr Parfitt. He peered at you with
bright, inquisitive eyes and asked you rather tersely what you
wanted. He was never obsequious to his customers; he always
seemed reluctant to sell anything; and indeed he had been known   15
to weep at parting with a fine old Welsh dresser which, he said,
was his proudest possession. His tears weren't faked; though the
dresser was. He was indeed proud of it, and he grieved to part with
it, for he had spent long days and nights fashioning it, with skill
and ingenuity and loving care, out of some odd bits of old, dark   20
oak which he'd picked up at a sale.

Mr Parfitt was probably the best carpenter in three counties,
and he had a right to be proud of his job, which was the most difficult in all the carpenter's trade. It was much more difficult, for
example, for Mr Parfitt to fake a Chippendale chair than it had   25
been for Thomas Chippendale to make the original; but I assure
you that Mr Parfitt would make you a very passable Chippendale
chair for about ten guineas. An expert could detect the forgery;
but he would have to be a real expert, for Mr Parfitt knew all the
old tricks, and had a few new ones of his own. For instance, if you   30
bought, in his shop, one of those convex mirrors, period about
1800, which are much sought after, and you took the precaution
of taking out the glass, you would find behind it, separating it
from the frame, a sheet from a newspaper bearing the correct date.
And if you were an old junk merchant you would be aware that   35
you could always get a few shillings from Mr Parfitt for a bundle
of newspapers dated round about 1800.

Not only was Mr Parfitt a fine craftsman, but he was also something of a pioneer. He discovered, long before anybody else the
enormous possibilities of Elmbury's tourist trade. Here was El   40
Dorado, lying at every tradesman's doorstep; but nobody realized it until Mr Parfitt began to sell curios which had 'local associations' to the visitors who came in summer to see the Abbey.
Soon others imitated him, and there grew up a brisk trade in
guide-books, picture postcards, drinking mugs inscribed 'A Pres-   45
ent from Elmbury', and even in pink sticks of Elmbury rock. But
Mr Parfitt, as befitted the discoverer of this El Dorado, continued
to reap the greatest riches from it, ever mining deeper into the tou-
rists' pockets and finding new deposits of gold.

JOHN MOORE, *Portrait of Elmbury* (Collins)

MULTIPLE CHOICE QUESTIONS

After reading each of the following questions, choose the ONE correct answer, and indicate it by writing down the letter that stands for it.

From Section A

1 To 'discredit' an article (l. 3) is to
   A make it appear worthless
   B notice the imperfections of it
   C regard it as out of fashion
   D underestimate the value of it
   E pretend to ignore it

2 'A ring' (l. 8) is a group of traders
   A wishing to buy the same things
   B resolved not to pay absurdly high prices
   C secretly acting together
   D united in a legal partnership
   E with common interests

3 A practice that is 'ethically sound' (l. 10) would be
   A apparently honest
   B completely moral
   C generally accepted among professional people
   D classed as tricks of the trade
   E conventional and respectable

4 In the first two paragraphs (ll. 1–15) the writer
   A is very critical of dealers' dishonesties
   B looks at the subject from the point of view of the lay purchaser
   C shows some sympathy for the dealer's genuine difficulties
   D admits that much might be said on both sides
   E analyses how a man's method of earning money affects his opinion of right and wrong

5 The writer classes the Smith Brothers as 'positively' dishonest because they
   A were careful to keep just inside the law
   B took advantage of the conceit and greed of other people
   C 'preyed mainly upon country cottagers and the inhabitants of the villages'
   D travelled to look deliberately for victims to cheat
   E showed considerable skill as deceitful actors

6 A dash is used in 1.27 after 'table' because the words that follow it
   A are, apparently, an afterthought added later
   B need to be emphasized
   C form a complete sentence on their own

    D show how hesitant Eric's speech was
    E were spoken in a mood of doubt and hesitation

7 The last sentence (ll. 45–50) stresses that the people whom the Smiths cheated were

    A unsuspecting
    B uninformed
    C overconfident
    D honest
    E gullible

From Section B

8 In describing the cottager as 'wise in the ways of crooks from London' (l. 15), the writer

    A is sarcastically making contemptuous fun of the cottager
    B stresses that the cottager will not fall for a simple trick
    C praises the cottager for showing some astuteness
    D admires the Smiths for overcoming so cautious an opponent
    E pretends to accept the cottager's view of himself

9 Which ONE of the following factors was *least* true of the Smiths' successful deceit?

    A Albert and Eric relied on their victims' simplicity
    B Albert appeared to study the table very carefully
    C Albert offered the cottager a cheque, which she felt clever to refuse
    D Albert apparently looked only casually at the valuable chest
    E Albert pretended not to have room for both chest and table

10 'Haggled' (l. 31) means

    A protested that the price was too low
    B hesitated about the price to charge
    C kept disputing about the price
    D tried to gain an unrealistic profit
    E drove a hard bargain

11 Which ONE of the following words or phrases gives the writer's real view of the Smith brothers?

    A 'Mr Smith's friend from London had cheated her' (ll. 42–3)
    B 'never broke the law once save when . . . . light' (ll. 49–51)
    C 'things that might happen to anybody' (ll. 51–2)
    D 'virtuous citizens' (l. 52)
    E 'great respecters of the Law' (l. 53)

12 A word that is used with a deliberately contemptuous colloquial tone is

    A 'worthless' (l. 41)
    B 'tricky' (l. 48)

    C 'copped' (l. 51)
    D 'practices' (l. 55)
    E 'faking' (l. 58)

13 Which ONE of the following words provides an example of irony, i.e.
    deliberately saying the opposite of what one means?
    A 'worthless' (l. 41)
    B 'cheated' (l. 43)
    C 'punished' (l. 47)
    D 'interfering' (l. 50)
    E 'virtuous' (l. 52)

14 Which ONE of the following remarks is *not* true?
    A they kept to the letter of the law
    B their deceit was in their buying more than in their selling
    C they hinted that Mr Parfitt, their rival, sold faked antiques
    D they were self-righteous
    E they were poor actors

15 In ll. 53–60 which of the following best fits the tone of voice in which
    the Smiths talked about their rival, Mr Parfitt?
    A they hinted darkly
    B they bluntly stated
    C they amusingly suggested
    D they protested indignantly
    E they exaggerated wildly

16 The tone of what the Smiths say about themselves (ll. 48–53) is
    A modest
    B exaggerated
    C insolent
    D self-righteous
    E puritanical

From Section C

17 Which ONE of the following was *not* among the reasons why the writer
    liked Mr Parfitt?
    A he always looked cheerful
    B the faking of antique furniture needed real skill
    C he was never servile and grovelling to his customers
    D his customers deserved to be cheated—presumably because of
       their ignorance
    E he enjoyed selling the things he had made

18 The view of Mr Parfitt which the Smith brothers gave (ll. 53–60 in Sec-
    tion B)
    A is fundamentally untrue

B describes his faults but omits his virtues

C shows that he, like the Smiths, kept the letter of the law

D expresses an indignation against Mr Parfitt's faults which the writer also felt

E uses words such as 'abominable' that stress the writer's disapproval of Mr Parfitt

19 'Inquisitive' (l. 13) means

    A kindly

    B eager

    C interested

    D curious

    E mercenary

20 It was necessary that Mr Parfitt's salesroom should be dark so that

    A he could economize on electric light

    B his old-fashioned furniture would be seen in a romantic atmosphere

    C the sun would not spoil the gloss on his furniture

    D customers could not detect his faked antiques

    E his weak eyes would not be harmed by bright sunlight

21 Mr Parfitt was a pioneer because

    A he imitated other shopkeepers in catering for tourists

    B he tried to attract tourists to his town

    C he was the first in the area to sell keepsakes for tourists

    D he resembled the explorers who hoped to find gold in El Dorado

    E he developed new types of furniture

TRADITIONAL QUESTIONS

Answer the following questions in your own words as far as possible. Questions marked with an asterisk should be answered *very briefly*, and in these answers complete sentences are not necessary.

From Section A

*1 Give in a single word or short phrase the meaning of *five* of the following words *as used in the passage*:

    i livelihood (l. 1)   **ii** discredit (l. 3)   **iii** ethically (l. 10)

    iv malpractices (l. 15)   **v** reconnaissance (l. 22)   **vi** rickety (l. 40)

    vii connoisseur (l. 47).

2 What two methods do the dealers employ to secure cheaply the articles which they wish to buy?

3 What is the difference between 'negatively honest' (l. 14) and 'positively dishonest' (l. 14)? Why could the methods of the Smith Brothers be classed as an example of positive dishonesty?

4 Show that the following metaphors convey more than plain statements: **i** 'They preyed mainly upon . . . . villages' (ll. 20–21) **ii** 'the Smith Brothers . . . . . . had long ago discovered and fleeced the last of them' (ll. 44–5). (See Part III of Paper I.)

5 Why did the Smith Brothers rely on making their money out of the most cunning country people?

6 What details are inserted in the story to show that Eric Smith was a good actor?

From Section B

*7 Give in a single word or short phrase the meaning of the following words *as used in the passage*:
i haggled (l. 31) **ii** remedy (l. 44) **iii** tricky (l. 48)
iv abominable (ll. 54–5).

*8 Quote two examples of slang words deliberately used to fit in with the atmosphere of the passage.

9 Do you think the word 'fearful' (l. 52) is used literally? Give a reason for your opinion.

10 Why does the writer use the word 'interfering' in line 50?

11 What is your opinion of the words 'upright' (l. 55) and 'blush' (l. 60) applied to the Smith Brothers?

12 Explain the term 'no names, no packdrill' (l. 56). Try to account for its origin.

13 In what ways were the appearance and methods of Albert Smith different from those of Eric?

From Section C

*14 Give in a single word or short phrase the meaning of *five* of the following words *as used in the passage*:
i austere (l. 8) **ii** wizened (l. 12) **iii** peered (l. 12) **iv** tersely
(l. 13) **v** obsequious (l. 14) **vi** passable (l. 27).

15 Why did the writer like Mr Parfitt better than he liked the Smiths?

16 In what ways did Mr Parfitt justify the hints made about him by the Smith Brothers?

17 Why is the writer justified in calling Mr Parfitt **i** 'a craftsman' (ll. 2–3) **ii** 'the best carpenter in three counties' (l. 22) **iii** 'a pioneer' (l. 39)?

18 Account for the following marks of punctuation:

  i the brackets before 'it' (l. 10) and after 'dark' (l. 10)   **ii** the semi-colons after 'customers' (l. 14) and after 'anything' (l. 15)   **iii** the semi-colon after 'faked' (l. 17)   **iv** the inverted commas before and after 'local associations' (ll. 42–3).

19 Explain the expression 'Here was El Dorado, lying at every tradesman's doorstep' (l. 41).

II. Writing English

Write on ONE of the following:

a Tell a story of village life which includes shady characters similar to those in the passage in Part I.
b How is 'progress' destroying rural communities such as Elmbury?
c Tell the story of a village threatened by the construction of a motorway nearby. The villagers are divided in their opinions; some are in favour, some are not. Give arguments on both sides in the form of a dialogue.
d Sponsored walks.
e How holidaymakers spend their money.
f Antiques.
g How a camping holiday ended in disaster.
h Write a story, a description or an essay suggested by the illustration on page 36. (Your composition may be directly about the subject of the illustration, or may only take suggestions from it, but there must be some clear connection between the illustration and the composition.)

Suggestions for Projects, Assignments and Course Work

1 Write a criticism of books that you have read dealing with one of the following themes:

  i The family and home life **ii** Being the odd one out **iii** Man's struggle against the elements.

2 Write four chapters of a novel about space exploration. These chapters would deal with

  i The problems that had to be solved before a long space flight was necessary
  ii Choosing the men to take part
  iii Misadventures in mid-flight
  iv The landing on Mars.

3 Write two chapters describing a Utopia, an ideal state.
  These chapters should deal with two topics such as How Criminals are Treated, the Status of Women, the Type of Education given, Safety Precautions, the Choice of TV Programmes.

III. Using English

Punctuation

Revise uses of question mark and exclamation mark. Note the following examples:

    i 'How awkward you are!'   **ii** 'How do you do?'
    iii 'I don't know how you manage.'

    See Unit I, Part III, for suggestions about punctuation revision. The dictation of questions, exclamations and statements is particularly effective.

1 Account for the following marks of punctuation in the passage in Part I:

i the commas after 'fake' (l.A.5), 'broken' (l.A.5), 'pound' (l.A.5) and 'bob' (l.A. 6)   **ii** the inverted commas before and after 'ring' (l.A. 8)   **iii** the semi-colon after 'sound' (l.A. 11)   **iv** the inverted commas before 'whether' and after 'sell' (ll.A. 23–4)   **v** the full stop *outside* the inverted commas after 'sell' (l.A. 24)   **vi** the colon after 'cunning' (l.A. 46)   **vii** the dashes before 'since' (l.B. 26) and after 'table' (l.B. 26)   **viii** the colon after 'light' (l.B. 51).

2 Punctuate the following passage:

every man woman and child took part in the search armed with sticks and pangas they beat into the thickets climbed the trees and peered into the interstices of walls and roofs heaps of fallen cashew leaves were raked over an improbable refuge for a green mamba which is habitually arboreal but a likely one for a spitting cobra or gaboon viper and there could be no certainty of the snake's identity yet and the thick red dust round the hut of death was examined minutely for tracks but none was found it seemed as though the snake had escaped by the way it came

Grammar and Usage

3 Pick out and state the kind of all the words used as adjectives and pronouns in the passage in Question 2 of Part III.

4 Correct the following sentences where necessary. Give reasons for your corrections.

i There was hardly nobody who didn't attend.
ii Mr Brown was just as anxious to catch the burglars as the policemen.
iii Looking down from the cliff a rough sea came into view.
iv You must be tired; lay down and sleep.
v Juries need no longer be quite unanimous in their verdict.

Spelling and Dictionary Work

5 The following words are incomplete. The dots indicate a letter or letters missing. The number of dots bears no relationship to the number of letters missing. Rewrite the words spelling them correctly.

i ir . . . sponsible   **ii** illeg . . . ble   **iii** con . . . ientious   **iv** fo . . . head
v mi . . . use   **vi** mi . . . pell   **vii** di . . . atisfaction
viii volcan . . . s   **ix** rep . . . tition   **x** daf . . . dil
xi tyran . . . cal   **xii** ex . . . rcise   **xiii** criti . . . ism   **xiv** supers . . . de
xv notic . . . ble   **xvi** ex . . . gerate.

6 Look at the spelling of the following words, and then try to formulate a rule for the spelling of words when 'ness' or 'less' is added:

i greenness   **ii** useless   **iii** tailless   **iv** brainless   **v** suddenness
Would you use hyphens in any of these words?

Style and Appreciation

7   *Four Haiku on the Inland Sea*

Morning
Are clouds or mountains
Floating in the island air
Half sea, half heaven?

Spring
Our boat softly swims
In falling cherry petals.
The fresh spray is pink.

Autumn
Each drifting island
Leans its lonely pine, and red
Maples fan dark glens.

Evening
In the amber dusk
Each island dreams its own night.
The sea swarms with gold.

JAMES KIRKUP

Haiku are Japanese poems consisting of stanzas of three lines, each stanza containing seventeen syllables. Notice the balance of the poem: Morning and Evening, Spring and Autumn. Try to compose your own Haiku, describing some scene with which you are familiar.

Books to read

Brensham Village	John Moore
At Night All Cats Are Grey	Patrick Boyle
Hath the Rain a Father?	Juanita Casey
The Heat of the Sun	Sean O'Faolain
The Man Who Doubted	Jack Cope
The Golden Apples of the Sun	Ray Bradbury
The Terminal Beach	J. G. Ballard
The Frontiers of the Sea	Peter Ustinov
Ring of Bright Water	Gavin Maxwell
My Turn to Make the Tea	Monica Dickens

Unit 4

I. Reading and Understanding

Read the following passage (which for your convenience has been divided into two sections) and then answer the questions.

THE WORLD FOOD PROGRAMME

[A] No-one really likes charity. It is a great deal more satisfactory to be given the opportunity to earn one's daily bread; and if, by so doing, one can create a continuing means of livelihood, more jobs, and better living conditions for one's community, that is more satisfactory still. It is on this premise that the World Food   5
Programme bases most of its operations.

But how can a man born of unemployed, undernourished parents, in the depths of poverty that pervades the shanty towns adjoining Latin American cities, or displaced people's camps in .
Africa and Asia, begin to get so much as one little toe on the   10
ladder of opportunity? Someone must help, someone who understands that both food and employment are fundamental to his need.

Most thinking people must have remarked at some time or other that it doesn't make sense for half the population of the   15
world to be in need of better food while governments and farmers elsewhere are worried by surpluses. For a number of years, until recently, North America and Australia had too much wheat. Japan had too much rice. Similarly the EEC rapidly built a butter 'mountain' in its short history.   20

It was an awareness of the cruel paradox of a world with surpluses and starvation that prompted the setting up of the World Food Programme by the United Nations and also by the Food and Agriculture Organization. Its organizers realized that it could be useful both to developed and developing countries. It could re-   25
move surpluses in such a way that they did not upset normal trading or threaten the livelihood of farmers in donor countries, and then use these commodities to feed people and aid development in underprivileged areas.

So how does the World Food Programme work and what has it   30
achieved?

Logically, the story starts with a pledging session. The donor countries, of which there have been a hundred and four over the years, pledge themselves to give a certain value during the succeeding two years. Most of these pledges are honoured by gifts of food, but countries which do not produce food surplus to their own needs pledge money to finance the administration and shipping of the food given by others.   35

Meanwhile, the WFP staff in Rome get requests from countries which would like to receive this food aid. Some of these are emergency requests—when earthquake, hurricane, flood, drought or pestilence strike, or political upheavals cause a new wave of refugees. Of course, WFP respond to these, but they represent no more than a quarter of its aid in any one year. The real objective is to aid constructive development, and so to build a bulwark against the everyday disaster of having little food to eat, no work to go to, no dignity to uphold.   40

So the WFP staff are responsive to requests from governments who want initial help to develop new lands for farming, to build roads, to terrace hillsides and plant the terraces with fruit and nut trees, to provide irrigation, and so on. The government of the would-be recipient country has to put forward what is considered to be a worthwhile and workable scheme and, if this is accepted, WFP agree to supply food to a certain value for a specified period of years (usually three to five). Usually the food is for the people; sometimes it is for their farm livestock.   45

                                                                    50

                                                                    55

[B]   Recently, I visited a hill village in the Troodos area of Cyprus on a day when food was being distributed. The people came smiling with their sacks and their donkeys to collect the food that they had earned. Each man, or a member of his family if he was away working in the fields, came to scrutinize the list which set out how much work had been done and how much wheat, flour or other commodity was, therefore, due.   5

In this case, the project was meant to conserve soil and moisture on the hillsides by building stone walls and terracing them, then planting almonds and improved varieties of grapes and other fruit that would eventually yield an income for the villagers.   10

A very common form of project is that which helps to settle displaced farmers. For example, the building of the Aswan Dam in Egypt has made possible the development and irrigation of vast new lands so that the country's desperately over-populated cultivated land can be extended. But what are the new settlers to live on until the virgin land bears full fruit? The World Food Programme helps the government to provide an answer by giving food.   15

In all cases, the WFP organisation is responsible for delivering the food to the recipient country, but then the country's govern-   20 ment must take over. Local administration must transport, store and distribute the food.

It is common to hear people in Britain express concern, or downright disbelief, about whether aid reaches those for whom it is intended. In the complex situations in which some aid is dis- 25 tributed it would be miraculous if some supplies did not go astray, but in the case of WFP development projects, a very careful check is kept by locally or regionally based staff and by teams of expert visiting evaluators. A project is not supported by WFP unless the available administration appears to be satisfactory and it is cer- 30 tainly not continued if the intended results are not being achieved.

About one-third of World Food Programme food goes to the so-called vulnerable groups in under-nourished com- munities—pregnant and nursing mothers and school children. In these circumstances, too, there are periodic assessments of pro- 35 gress to make sure that the food is being properly used. And the hope all the while is that *these* children will grow up to live in a world in which they are given full opportunity to support and feed themselves. Then the World Food Programme will no longer be wanted. Its concept will be obsolete. But the human race is a very 40 long way from achieving that happy state.

MARY CHERRY, 'The World Food Programme' (*The Lady*)

MULTIPLE CHOICE QUESTIONS

After reading each of the following questions, choose the ONE correct answer, and indicate it by writing down the letter that stands for it.

From Section A

1 The main idea of the first two paragraphs (ll. 1–13) is that many people
   A feel offended by people who offer them gifts
   B are prevented from rising in the world by the poverty of their sur- roundings
   C need to be given both food and the chance to earn their living
   D feel their pride hurt if they are given charity
   E need to feel that those who are in a position to help them really understand their situation

2 A 'premise' (l. 5) is
   A an ideal that motivates action
   B the first step that will ultimately lead to greater successes
   C the assumption that progress is still usually possible
   D a statement that is assumed to be true
   E the first instalment of improvement from which better things will grow

3 Paragraph II (ll. 7–13)

A answers an objection that some readers may raise to Paragraph I

B guards against the possibility that you have read Paragraph I rather carelessly

C contradicts the idea of Paragraph I

D is more optimistic than Paragraph I

E adopts a more confident tone than Paragraph I

4 Paragraph IV (ll. 21–9) emphasizes that since surpluses (e.g. of butter) exist, therefore aid programmes

A may promote overproduction of some goods

B put the interests of the producers before those of the consumers

C could interfere with more normal types of trade

D could very well upset ordinary methods of trade

E will help the givers as well as the receivers

5 A 'paradox' (l. 21) is

A an apparent contradiction

B a serious injustice

C a tragedy that can be prevented

D a result of man's selfish greed

E a moral to be learnt by experience

6 'A pledging session' (l. 32) means that the richer countries

A give their word that they will hand over their surpluses to poorer countries

B promise to give aid up to a certain value

C undertake to provide certain quantities of food

D find ways of preventing overproduction of certain foods

E forecast their own production of essential foods

7 The main aim of the WFP is to

A meet the needs created by unexpected crises such as hurricanes

B give food to those nations that need it

C find a way of helping poorer nations to cope with emergencies

D assist countries which are hit by unusual disasters such as earthquakes

E help the poorer nations to help themselves

8 In l. 41 which ONE of the following methods of punctuation would be clearly wrong?

A requests when earthquake

B requests. When earthquake

C requests, when earthquake

D requests (when earthquake

E requests:—when earthquake

9 Which ONE of the following phrases is to be taken literally (not figuratively or metaphorically)?

A 'No-one really likes charity' (l. 1)

B 'in the depths of poverty' (l. 8)

C 'they did not upset normal trading (ll. 26–7)

D when earthquake, hurricane, flood, drought or pestilence strike' (ll. 41–2)

E 'political upheavals cause a new wave of refugees' (l. 42)

10 The word 'bulwark' (l. 45) compares the aid programme to a

A defence against attack (e.g. a wall or an earthwork)

B sure method of prevention

C temporary solution to a pressing problem

D type of insurance policy

E sort of germ-killer to prevent danger

11 The phrase 'no dignity to uphold' (l. 47) stresses the need to

A provide food as a first priority

B support the authority of the ruling classes in poor countries

C begin schemes of aid that are constructive

D preserve the self-respect of those whom one is helping

E avoid too much interference with the internal politics of poorer countries

12 WFP's plans for underdeveloped countries emphasize the need to

A develop types of fruit tree that will resist disease

B extend the area of land fit for cultivation

C remove or flatten out the tops of hills

D provide food for farm animals

E increase the use of agricultural machinery in primitive countries

13 'Initial' help means help (l. 49)

A that is much needed

B in meeting the cost

C in the beginning

D for a considerable time

E in the long run

14 The passage avoids emotional phrases as much as possible. One of its few emotional phrases is:

A 'It is on this premise that the World Food Programme bases most of its operations' (ll. 5–6)

B 'Someone must help, someone who understands that both food and employment are fundamental to his need' (ll. 11–13)

C 'Similarly the EEC rapidly built a butter "mountain" in its short history' (ll. 19–20)

     D 'the cruel paradox of a world with surpluses and starvation . . . prompted the setting up of the World Food Programme' (ll. 21–3)

     E 'Most of these pledges are honoured by gifts of food' (ll. 35–6)

15 An argument which Section A includes, but which is opposed to its main argument, is that

     A it is more dignified and self-satisfying to be helped to produce food than to be given it

     B a man who is unemployed and whose parents are poor finds it very difficult to help himself

     C it is illogical for half of mankind to go hungry while farmers in other countries produce surpluses

     D the main aim of WFP is to help the backward countries to increase their eventual productiveness

     E some countries help WFP with gifts of food; others pay for the cost of transporting the food

From Section B

16 The major purpose of ll. 1–7 is to stress that the villagers in the Troodos area of Cyprus

     A studied closely the distribution list of the various foods

     B received only a little food for the work they had done

     C were pleased that they had worked hard to deserve the food

     D were able to send substitutes if they were still working

     E smiled with gratitude when given the food

17 The farmers in Egypt (as distinct from those in Cyprus) were

     A in more immediate need of food from WFP

     B less typical of recipients in most countries

     C learning how to produce more food from less land

     D more dependent upon their own government to distribute supplies

     E more happy and confident about their future

18 Which ONE of the following does WFP *not* do?

     A it transports food to the country which needs it

     B it helps the local government administration to distribute the food

     C it checks whether the local government administration distributes the food fairly

     D it discontinues plans that do not produce satisfactory results

     E it encourages the local farmers to develop more suitable strains of fruit

19 The theory that aid fails to reach those who need it is

     A untrue

     B paradoxical

     C amusing

     D illusory

     E exaggerated

20 'Its concept' (l. 40) means the

    A necessity for WFP
    B idea of WFP existing at all
    C opportunities provided by WFP
    D target that WFP hopes to attain
    E first founding of WFP

TRADITIONAL QUESTIONS

Answer the following questions in your own words as far as possible. Questions marked with an asterisk should be answered *very briefly*; and in these answers complete sentences are not necessary.

From Section A

*1 Give in a single word or short phrase the meaning of *five* of the following words *as used in the passage*:

    i fundamental (l. 12)   **ii** donor (l. 27)   **iii** commodities (l. 28)   **iv** logically (l. 32)   **v** responsive (l. 48)   **vi** recipient (l. 52)   **vii** specified (l. 54).

2 Explain the meaning of two of the following:

    i 'underprivileged areas' (l. 29)   **ii** 'a pledging session' (l. 32)   **iii** 'initial help' (l. 49).

3 What is the 'cruel paradox' referred to in line 21? Explain in your own words.

4 Show how the following figurative expressions convey more than plain statements:

    i 'But how can a man . . . get so much as one little toe on the ladder of opportunity' (ll. 7–11)   **ii** a butter 'mountain' (l. 19)   **iii** 'a new wave of refugees' (l. 42).

5 What is the difference between 'emergency requests' (l. 40) and 'constructive development' (l. 45)?

6 Why should governments and farmers be worried by surpluses?

7 How might 'normal trading' (l. 26) be upset, do you suppose?

From Section B

*8 Give in a single word or short phrase the meaning of *four* of the following words *as used in the passage:*

    i scrutinize (l. 5)   **ii** virgin (l. 17)   **iii** complex (l. 25)   **iv** evaluators (l. 29)   **v** vulnerable (l. 33).

9 Explain the meaning of the following:

    i 'Local administration' (l. 21)   **ii** 'regionally based staff' (l. 28)   **iii** 'periodic assessments' (l. 35).

10 Give in your own words the meaning of 'Its concept will be obsolete' (l. 40).

From the whole passage

11 write two paragraphs summarizing the information given in the passage about:

    i the reasons for the setting up of the World Food Programme *and*

    ii the ways in which the World Food Programme helps needy countries.

Each paragraph should not exceed 85 words in length.

II. Writing English

Write a composition on ONE of the following subjects:

a Imagine you live in a hill village in the Troodos area of Cyprus (Section B, paragraph 1). From the information given try to describe your daily life and contrast it with the life of a teenager in Britain or in another comparatively rich country.

b   'Where I spat in the harbour the oranges were bobbing

      All salted and sodden, with eyes in their rinds;

      The sky was all black where the coffee was burning,

      And the rust of the freighters had reddened the tide.'

These lines from a poem by Randall Jarrell describe the dumping and burning of food surplus to a country's requirements in order to keep prices up in the 1930s. Do you think the WFP is a solution to this, or should there be an entirely different approach by the nations of the world?

c Famine.

d The hole in the road.

e Give your arguments for and/or against membership of the Common Market. Will economic unity lead to political unity, and is this desirable? Is such an organization a step towards world peace?

f Family allowances were instituted to help parents look after large families. If the present fear is a 'population explosion', should not all family allowances and tax concessions be withdrawn, or at least decreased as the number of children increases?

g Charities and the Welfare State.

Suggestions for Projects, Assignments and Course Work

1 The Village—trace the history of a village, real or imaginary, from its beginning to its extinction in the 20th century.

2 Planning (or following) a Nature Trail.

3 Beachcombing—in life and books and films.

III. Using English

Punctuation

Revise uses of inverted commas (speech, including the comma with direct speech; titles of books etc.—note exceptions to this use; quotations).
   N.B. Dialogue in plays.

1 Justify the following marks of punctuation in the passage in Part I:
   i the commas before and after 'until recently' (ll.A. 17–18)   **ii** the inverted commas before and after 'mountain' (l.A. 20)   **iii** the commas after 'earthquake, hurricane, flood' (l.A. 41)   **iv** the hyphen between 'would' and 'be' (l.A. 52)   **v** the commas before and after 'too' (l.B. 35).

2 Punctuate the following passage:

   he took the mutton off the gridiron and gravely handed it round we all took some but our appreciation of it was gone and we merely made a show of eating it as we severally pushed away our plates he noiselessly removed them and set on the cheese he took that too when it was done with cleared the table piled everything on the dumb waiter gave us our wine glasses and of his own accord wheeled the dumb waiter into the pantry all this was done in a perfect manner and he never raised his eyes from what he was about yet his very elbows when he had his back towards me seemed to teem with the expression of his fixed opinion that i was extremely young can i do anything more sir

Grammar and Usage

3 Words used as adjectives tell us about nouns, e.g. in the passage in Part I, 'daily' in line A. 2 tells us about 'bread'. There are different kinds of adjectives to do different jobs: demonstrative adjectives point out; adjectives of quantity say how many or how much; adjectives of quality say of what kind; possessive adjectives say to whom something belongs. Pick out three examples of each kind and say which noun is described in each case.

4 Use the following words in separate sentences as (a) adjectives (b) pronouns:
   i these   **ii** much   **iii** his   **iv** that   **v** any.

Spelling and Dictionary Work

5 Doubling consonants
   Words of ONE syllable:

   tip—tipping, tipped; step—stepping, stepped; steep—steeper, steeped; dust—dusty, duster; walk—walking, walker.

   Words of MORE than one syllable:

   óffer—offered, offering; ópen—opened, opening; preférred, preferring; occúr—occurred, occurring; lével—levelling.

Study the above examples and then try to construct rules for doubling or not doubling the final consonant.

Try adding -ing to the following: gallop, begin, trot, fool, dig, benefit, tap, overlap, leap, fulfil.

6 The following words are incomplete. The dots indicate a letter or letters missing. The number of dots bears no relationship to the number of letters missing. Write out the words, spelling them correctly.

i Feb . . . . . ary ii accom . . . . . date iii bu . . . . . ness (trade)
iv hum . . . . . rous v rec . . . . . ve vi f . . . . . teen (14)
vii sep . . . . . rate viii notic . . . . . able ix benefi . . . . . ed (past tense of 'benefit') x for . . . . . gn (alien).

Style and appreciation

7 Look up the word 'paradox' (l. A.21) in your dictionary. How does this figure of speech achieve its effect? Is the following a paradox? 'A life of ease is a difficult pursuit.'

8 In presenting a case for the World Food Programme, does the writer try to avoid emotional words and appeals? Give some evidence to support your answer.

9 Show that one of the devices used by the writer to put her case is the question and answer method.

10 The first sentence states: 'No-one really likes charity.' Show by reference to later sentences that this idea is continued throughout the extract.

Books to read.

Love on the Dole	Walter Greenwood
Aneurin Bevan	Michael Foot
The Stars Look Down	A. J. Cronin
The War of the Worlds	H. G. Wells
Aku-Aku	Thor Heyerdahl
Goodbye to All That	Robert Graves
The Grapes of Wrath	John Steinbeck
Lucky Jim	Kingsley Amis
A Town Like Alice	Nevil Shute
The Red Badge of Courage	Stephen Crane

Unit 5

I. Reading and Understanding

Read the following passage (which for your convenience has been divided into three sections) and then answer the questions.

FOOTBALL HOOLIGANISM

[A] Undoubtedly the most damaging aspect of our football at the moment is hooliganism. Other facets of the matter may be debated; this violence is solely harmful. Mr Dennis Follows, when he was secretary of the Football Association, diagnosed it accurately, though his suggested remedy was obviously unacceptable 5
when he advocated the banning of spectators under the age of eighteen from football grounds.

His idea was rejected for valid human reasons. Saturday has replaced the old Sunday morning as the working man's time of glory. The football match, core of Saturday, is, for many orderly 10
youthful citizens as well as the unruly, the compensation for a week of monotonous, depressing work and, often, dispiriting family life. Mr Follows identified the specifically disruptive adolescent element.

On the other hand, many of his critics appeared to think that 15
the youngsters in question were simply football followers enthusiastically supporting their own teams. If that were the whole matter it would be relatively easy to adjust: but it is not. Apparently it is not generally realized that many of these young men drink heavily on their football match 'day out'. The youngest of 20
them—quite early teenagers—can be seen buying drink in the public-houses near many of the large grounds; it is simpler, safer, and more profitable for publicans to serve them than to ask their age or refuse. It may be accepted from one who has now twice been forced to defend himself against their mindless violence, that 25
a mob of drunken fifteen- or sixteen-year-olds is frighteningly illogical, unpredictable, and potentially violent.

A significant statistic of public reaction shows that in a recent year Boxing Day attendances at League matches were 300,000 lower than in the previous year. This, on a fine day for the season, 30
could not be explained away by the postponement of one Second

and one Fourth Division match, the general quality of play, or competition from television.

The effect of hooliganism is almost certainly wider than has generally been accepted. It is not limited to driving away specta-   35
tors who used to watch from the terraces, who are not prepared to take the risk of violence there, but cannot afford grandstand seats. It is increasingly clear that a considerable number of people, who used to travel by train to 'their' team's away matches, or from areas without first-class football, no longer do so because of the   40
atmosphere created by young 'supporters' in trains and at railway stations.

[B]   A number of clubs protested at Mr Follows's suggestion, which would estrange their regular supporters of the future at a formative stage in their loyalty. Yet many of them must have seen some economic merit in his proposals. By comparison with their figures even of a dozen years ago, many League clubs now pay   5
such a vastly increased sum for police, specifically to control the teenage element at their matches, that it barely exceeds the revenue from their admission payments. Indeed, if the loss through the number of older people driven away were taken into account, they might show a deficit on the arrangement.   10

If its administrators are genuinely concerned with the future of English football, they must accept the fact that the game has become identified, not with teenagers—that point should be made sharply clear—but with teenage hooligans. They are not an age-group but a social phenomenon. They have taken football merely   15
as a convenient—indeed, inviting—environment. In other circumstances they might have chosen Rugby League, dirt-track racing, boxing, or all-in wrestling as their stamping ground.

Until the question is solved it is not simply a static, but a constantly intensifying, irritant on the body of football. For many of   20
the youngsters, especially when they travel to an away fixture, the football match is simply the justification for a day out, away from the restrictions of the town where they live and are known. While football may attempt to deal with the problem, others are involved—some of whom neglect their responsibilities. Schools   25
and youth establishments of various kinds could, through a couple of journeys by staff members, identify and subsequently correct or restrain their pupils who regularly form violent Saturday gangs in other towns.

[C]   More regrettable and ominous is the attitude of British Rail. On normal weekdays their trains are safe and orderly. On Satur-

days and Bank Holiday football days, however, they appear
increasingly to abandon them to the teenage bands who prowl the
corridors like dogs through an Arab village, offering obscenity, 5
threats and violence to other travellers, in the proven certainty
that they will not be checked. On some 'football specials' a degree
of order is maintained through Supporters' Club organizations,
weight of opinion, and occasional police. On other trains, there is
no control at all. 10

It is important to these adolescents that the football ground,
the railway station and the train have in common the advantages
of both a public and a private place. They may go to any of them
freely, so long as they pay—and generally they have plenty of
money—but they are not subject to the disciplines which apply in 15
a public place. If they behaved in the mass hysterical fashion of the
terraces in the streets of a town, they would be broken up and
moved on; but the responsibilities of police engaged for special
duties at football grounds are roughly limited to the prevention or
reduction of violence. Railway stations or trains are policed by the 20
Transport Commission. The normal civil police only enter railway property on VIP occasions, or at the invitation of the railway
authority. The Railway Police is a small force; few of them are to
be seen at the major termini when the football crowds are in full
cry. 25

The alternative is the state of affairs which exists on the New
York subway where, outside specific hours, the civic and transport authorities surrender control to violent elements.

A brief study of the fixture lists would show the British Rail
executives what their train crews know in advance—the trains 30
that will carry the mobs each Saturday. It should not then be
beyond their contrivance, by policing or by closing connecting
doors between coaches, to afford peaceful passengers peace.

This whole danger can only be dealt with by concerted action.
The football clubs may, legally—though not morally nor effec- 35
tively—discharge their responsibility by engaging police for
special duty inside the ground while the crowds are there; the
civil police by shepherding them—sometimes—from the ground
to the entrance of the nearest railway station. At that point the
system breaks down. Supervision is required which can only be 40
provided by cooperation.

In recent years British Rail has increasingly backed away from
the concept of social responsibility in most branches of its activities. When action is eventually enforced—outside manpower will
have to be employed. 45

Some method and manning ought soon to be planned, for the

present confrontations in trains cannot long continue without some grave, criminally violent incident.

JOHN ARLOTT, 'Like Dogs through Arab Villages' (*The Guardian*)

MULTIPLE CHOICE QUESTIONS

After reading each of the following questions, choose the ONE correct answer, and indicate it by writing down the letter that stands for it.

From Section A

1 Mr Follows was correct (according to John Arlott) in
  A realizing that football hooligans are normally under eighteen
  B wishing to ban spectators under eighteen
  C advocating severe action against hooligans
  D appreciating how monotonous their weekday work is for many adolescents
  E understanding what Saturday means to working men

2 'Facets of the matter' (l. 2) means
  A details of the argument
  B circumstances of the time
  C prominent features of the debate
  D aspects of football
  E characteristics of adolescents

3 The purpose of the semi-colon in line 3 is to
  A indicate that the grammar of the sentence is incomplete
  B introduce a phrase that explains the first part of the sentence
  C underline the contrast between the two halves of the sentence
  D mark the switch from discussing causes to discussing consequences
  E include an example of the facets to be debated

4 'Valid' (l. 8) means
  A substantial
  B effective
  C sound
  D precise
  E undisputed

5 The main idea of paragraph 2 (ll. 8–14) is that young workers
  A often have monotonous tasks in an industrial society
  B need to watch football on Saturdays as compensation for a dull life
  C often form disruptive groups in football crowds
  D discourage responsible teenagers from watching matches
  E often fail to fit smoothly into the lives of their families

6 The main theme of paragraph 3 (ll. 15–27) is that

    A many young football supporters drink too heavily before the match

    B the problem of hooliganism is not easy to solve

    C many teenagers are quite irrational in their behaviour

    D the idea put forward by Mr Follows has been misunderstood

    E John Arlott is talking from personal experience

7 'Accepted' (l. 24) means taken as

    A welcome

    B approved

    C true

    D probable

    E adequate

8 Lines 28–42 stress that young hooligans

    A are difficult for the police to control

    B do less to reduce crowds than competition from television does

    C make older spectators unwilling to stand in the cheaper parts of grounds

    D make a wide variety of other spectators unwilling to attend matches

    E do a lot of damage to railway trains and stations

9 In view of the points made by John Arlott it is illogical that he does not advocate

    A preventing television companies from screening scenes of crowd violence

    B shutting public houses during the hours preceding a football match

    C banning all spectators under eighteen from watching football

    D building barriers to prevent hooligans from invading the actual playing pitches

    E raising the age at which it becomes legal to drink in a public house

10 The sentence 'This, on a fine day . . . . . .' (l. 30) means that the smallness of the crowds was due to the

    A opportunity to see the best games on television

    B potential spectators' fear of hooliganism

    C postponement of two matches

    D unusual circumstances of the day

    E decline in the attractiveness of the football played

11 'Atmosphere' (l. 41) means the

    A game's mental and moral surroundings

    B air that surrounds the earth

    C feeling of unpleasantness created by hooligans

    D frightening threat of imminent violence

    E interference with peaceful spectators

From Section B

12 Mr Follows's critics believed that his proposal would

    A reduce the profit made by football clubs

    B place too heavy a burden upon the police

    C discourage older spectators from attending matches

    D prevent young supporters from developing enthusiasm for their teams

    E provide only a short-term solution of the problem

13 Which ONE of the following remarks about the punctuation is *not* correct?

    A the *comma* after 'suggestion' (l. 1) shows that the following clause defines 'suggestion'

    B the two commas in ll. 6–7 bracket off the phrase 'specifically . . . matches' as a less important aside

    C the dashes in ll. 13–14 introduce an idea that is not made a part of the grammatical structure of the sentence

    D the dashes in l. 16 introduce a word that is stronger than 'convenient'

    E the commas in ll. 19–20 show that 'static' and 'intensifying' both describe 'irritant'

14 'To estrange' (l. 2) their potential future supporters is to

    A challenge them

    B neglect them

    C turn them into enemies

    D penalize them financially

    E underestimate them

15 Which ONE of the following points is *not* made in ll. 11–29?

    A teenagers who are hooligans are attracted to football matches, especially away from home

    B the majority of teenagers cannot fairly be classed as hooligans

    C if other sports had provided circumstances so appealing to hooligans, such sports, and not football, might have attracted them

    D the problem of football hooliganism continues to get worse

    E agencies outside football are trying their best to reduce hooliganism

16 In ll. 25–9 Arlott recommends using teachers as a kind of

    A security guard

    B detective

    C sentry

    D caretaker

    E policeman

From Section C

17 'Ominous' (l. 1) means

    A foreshadowing disaster
    B unfavourable
    C completely hostile
    D defeatist
    E irresponsible

18 The word 'however' in l. 3 shows that the sentence beginning on 'Saturdays and Bank Holiday football days'

    A continues the idea of the previous sentence
    B follows on logically from the previous sentence
    C gives an example of the thing mentioned in the previous sentence
    D is contrasted with the idea of the previous sentence
    E is on quite a different subject from the previous sentence

19 'It is important to' (these adolescents) (l.11) means in the context that it

    A matters intensely to them
    B is valued by them
    C is attractive to them
    D is noticed by them
    E gives them the chance to misbehave

20 John Arlott argues that the senior officials of British Rail

    A worry too much about football hooliganism
    B are right not to panic about football hooliganism
    C fail to take appropriate steps to deal with football hooliganism
    D rely too much on the normal civil police
    E cannot be held responsible for the behaviour of football supporters

21 The phrase 'are in full cry' (l. 24) compares the football crowds to

    A wolves
    B foxhounds
    C Arab dogs
    D retreating soldiers
    E howling babies

22 Section C gives most emphasis to football hooliganism as a problem for

    A the football clubs
    B both the clubs and the police
    C the politicians
    D the railway authorities
    E both the clubs and British Rail

TRADITIONAL QUESTIONS

Answer the following questions in your own words as far as possible. Questions marked with an asterisk should be answered *very briefly*, and in these answers complete sentences are not necessary.

From Section A

*1 Give in a single word or short phrase the meaning of *five* of the following words *as used in the passage*:
    i facets (l. 2)   ii diagnosed (l. 4)   iii advocated (l. 6)   iv valid (l. 8)
    v mindless (l. 25)   vi potentially (l. 27).

2 To what did the secretary of the Football Association attribute football hooliganism?

3 What was the F.A. secretary's remedy for hooliganism at football matches? Why is it unacceptable?

4 The football match is described as 'the core of Saturday' (l. 10). Explain this expression.

5 What, according to the writer, distinguishes the enthusiasm of football followers from football hooliganism?

6 What is a 'significant statistic' (l. 28)?

7 Are the effects of hooliganism confined to the football grounds? If not, where else are its effects felt?

8 Why is the word 'supporters' (l. 41) in inverted commas?

From Section B

*9 Give in a single word or short phrase the meaning of *four* of the following words *as used in the passage*:
    i estrange (l. 2)   ii specifically (l. 6)   iii deficit (l. 10)
    iv static (l. 19)   v intensifying (l. 20).

10 What do you understand by the expressions   i 'a formative stage' (l. 3) and   ii 'economic merit' (l. 4)?

11 Teenage hooligans are not 'an age-group but a social phenomenon' (ll. 14–15). Explain this statement.

12 What is meant by the expression 'this stamping ground' (l. 18)? Try to suggest the origin of the expression.

13 The question of teenage hooliganism is an 'irritant on the body of football' (l. 20). Show how this figure of speech conveys the author's point of view more clearly than a plain statement.

14 Who, besides the football administrators, are in some way to blame for the behaviour of many teenage football supporters?

From Section C

*15 Give in a single word or short phrase the meaning of the following *as used in the passage*:

    i ominous (l. 1)   **ii** proven (l. 6)   **iii** executives (l. 30)
    iv contrivance (l. 32).

16 What are mobs of teenage rail travellers compared to? How effective is the comparison?

17 What does the writer mean when he says that football grounds, railway stations and trains have the 'advantages of both a public and a private place' (ll. 12–13)?

18 Why are police less effective against the violence of football hooligans than they are against other kinds of violence?

19 What suggestions does the writer make to counteract violence on trains?

From the Whole Passage

20 Summarize the passage in Part I in about 200 of your own words.

II. Writing English

Write on ONE of the following:

a Write a vivid account of a sporting fixture you attended or took part in. Make your account credible by giving details and descriptions of scene and characters.

b Account for the popularity of a hobby that involves collecting.

c. Horses.

d A Red Indian tribe has a privileged group within it which does everything by opposites: they wash in dirt, they dry themselves with water, they shiver in the sun, they say 'no' for 'yes'. Imagine that for one day in your own country you become a 'contrary'. Describe what happens.

e The end of the road. This can be a story or a description.

f Write a series of letters between two school friends (two letters from each) in the course of which plans for a holiday which they would take together are suggested, changed, argued about, and finally abandoned. Use the letter form in all four of the letters.

g Pop Festivals. Account for their popularity with some and unpopularity with others. Show how proper planning and organization of such events could lead to acceptance by a greater number of people.

h 'And no birds sing.'

i Write a story, a description or an essay suggested by the illustration above. (Your composition may be directly about the subject of the illustration, or may only take suggestions from it, but there must be some clear connection between the illustration and the composition.)

Suggestions for Projects, Assignments and Course Work

1 Canals—history in this country and/or other countries such as Holland—the life led by canal people—the decline of canals—the present need (for recreation and possibly horse-drawn transport). A description of a journey by water through this country or through Europe—illustrate with appropriate maps etc.

2 Make a study of one or two boys' or girls' magazines. Analyse their contents—stories, advertisements, illustrations, stories in pictures (words in 'balloons'), sport, 'free gifts', hobbies. Make suggestions for improvements in content and format. Why were the titles 'comic' and 'penny dreadful' given to early magazines for young people? Draw up a contents page for the magazine you would like to produce.

3 Choose an area you know well, preferably a rural area, and by consulting books in your school and local libraries, find out the origin of place

names. Deal with a few in detail, showing how certain place names reflect local and/or national history.

III. Using English

Revise uses of colon (before a list; to indicate balance between two halves of a sentence as in 'Speech is silver: silence is golden). Sometimes the colon is used to introduce direct speech. Note the pointer:—a combination of the colon and the dash, used to introduce a list.

Punctuation

1 Punctuate the following, which consists of eight unconnected sentences on different topics: I had lost my cap one of my slippers and my shirt was torn to rags the masts will be toppling over directly we sat by the fire and watched the rain through the window because the weather was fine we played tennis have you seen the evening paper he asked jim swung the gate open for breakfast he ate bacon and eggs marmalade and toast dont look now he exclaimed

2 Correct the punctuation of the following sentences where necessary, giving reasons for the changes you make:

   i The wine, that was poured from the bottle, was unfit to drink.
  ii St James's Park the home ground was flooded.
 iii I'm going home, you can do what you like.
  iv The customer asked whether the garage had any petrol?
   v 'Have you seen "The Taming of the Shrew?"' asked his friend.

Grammar and Usage

Revise prepositions and conjunctions.

3 The following proverbs are ambiguous; they can be interpreted in two ways. Explain the two meanings which can be attributed to each proverb.

  i Feed a cold and starve a fever. **ii** Ne'er cast a clout till May is out.

4 What is wrong with the following sentences? Rewrite them correctly.

  i Sadly the bus was driven away before the old lady could reach the bus stop. **ii** Running swiftly, the race was won by the youngest competitor.

Spelling and Dictionary Work

5 The following words are incomplete. The dots indicate a letter or letters missing. The number of dots bears no relation to the number of letters missing. Write out the words, spelling them correctly.

  i notic . . . . . ble   **ii** u . . . . . ecessary   **iii** m . . . . . rm . . . . . r
 iv mistak . . . . . ble   **v** curr . . . . . nt (electric)   **vi** sincer . . . . . y
(adverb) **vii** rou . . . . . (road)   **viii** lab . . . . . rer
 ix light . . . . . ing (thunder and)   **x** vil . . . . . n (scoundrel).

6 Use a dictionary to find out the derivation of the following words:

  i melancholy   **ii** handkerchief **iii** khaki **iv** robot
  v mugwump **vi** Vaseline **vii** bonfire **viii** acre **ix** hermit
  x petrol.

7 Look up the meaning of the following words and then use them in sentences:

  i momentum   **ii** morass **iii** veto **iv** delta **v** budget **vi** aerie.

Style and Appreciation

8 What makes the following expressions, all advertisements, effective?

  i We dye to live, while others live to die.
 ii Sleepwell bedding for the rest of your life.
 iii Anchoria (name of a seaside guest house).

9 Explain, and comment on, the following poems:

 i   *Heartbreak House*

        Shaw's Corner to let, unfurnished
        Your Irish wit made you bequeath
        This hideous dump to English dust?—
        Even in life we viewed you with
        A national mistrust.

        PATRIC DICKINSON, *The Scale of Things* (Chatto & Windus)

ii   *Historical Survey*

It seems odd
     That whenever man chooses
To play God—
     God loses.
          FELICIA LAMPORT, *Cultural Slag* (Victor Gollancz)

Books to read

Borstal Boy	Brendan Behan
To Sir, with Love	C. R. Braithwaite
In Hazard	Richard Hughes
The Man who Won the Pools	J. I. M. Stewart
There is a Happy Land	Keith Waterhouse
Autobiography of a Super-Tramp	W. H. Davies
Second Orbit	ed. G. D. Doherty
Joanna and Ulysses	M. Sarton
South Col	Wilfrid Noyce
The Hanging Tree	D. M. Johnson

Unit 6

Read the following passage (which for your convenience has been divided into two sections) and then answer the questions.

THE HISTORY OF THE TULIP

[A]   No classical author mentions a flower which can with any degree of probability be identified with the tulip, though one of the varieties which now grow wild in Italy is almost certainly indigenous and several kinds are not uncommon in Greece; no Western painting, pottery or textile earlier than the end of the six-   5
teenth century shows it; and the well-known 'Roman' mosaic which includes garden tulips is now generally agreed to be an eighteenth-century reconstruction.

   In the year 1554 Busbecq, Ambassador from the Emperor Ferdinand I to Suleiman the Magnificent, was on his way from   10
Adrianople to Constantinople when he observed 'an abundance of flowers everywhere—narcissus, hyacinths, and those which the Turks call *tulipam*—much to our astonishment, because it was almost mid-winter, a season unfriendly to flowers. Greece (it was part of the Turkish empire) abounds in narcissus and hyacinths   15
remarkable for their fragrance, which is so strong as to hurt those not used to it; the tulipam, however, have little or no smell, but are admired for the beauty and variety of their colours. The Turks pay great attention to the cultivation of flowers, and do not hesitate, although they are far from extravagant, to pay several aspers for   20
one that is beautiful. I received several presents of these flowers, which cost me not a little.'

   The fame of the flower spread quickly; in 1561 rich German bankers were growing it in Augsburg, and the following year an Antwerp merchant received a 'cargo' of bulbs from Con-   25
stantinople. From Flanders the tulip was introduced into its spiritual home, Holland; and about the year 1578 it reached England.

   The tulip was late in reaching France, where the religious wars had turned men's thoughts from the gentle pursuit of gardening, and there is no record of a bulb flowering there until 1608. But   30
soon after this, no woman of fashion would be seen in the spring without a bunch of rare blooms tucked into her low-cut dress, and

within a few years bulbs were changing hands for fantastic sums.
For one bulb of 'Mère brune' a miller agreed to part with his mill;
a young Frenchman expressed himself delighted at receiving for   35
his bride's dowry a single bulb of a rare tulip appropriately chris-
tened 'Mariage de ma fille'; while another enthusiast exchanged a
flourishing brewery, valued at 30 000 francs, for a bulb named
'Tulipe brasserie' in commemoration of the event. The craze
spread northwards through Flanders (where Rubens was busy   40
painting his second wife, Helena Fourment, in her new tulip
garden) to Holland, which was to be the stage for the most astonishing drama in the whole history of horticulture—the *Tulpen-
woede*, or Tulipomania.

[B]   The tulipomania was at its height between the years 1634
and 1637, but some time before this the enthusiasm of Dutch amateurs had already forced the prices of rare bulbs up to a ridiculous
figure. Of one named 'Semper Augustus', with a red and white
flower and blue-tinted base, Wassenaer wrote in 1623: 'No tulip   5
has been held in higher esteem, and one has been sold for thousands of florins; yet the seller was himself sold (so he said), for
when the bulb was lifted, he noticed two lumps on it which the
year following would have become two offsets, and so he was
cheated of two thousand florins.' These offsets, he adds, 'are the   10
interest, while the capital remains.'
Soon everyone who had a few square yards of back garden was
growing bulbs. The outlay was small—a few breeder tulips; the
prizes were enormous. Hand in hand with tulip-growing went
speculation, which, says Beckmann, 'was followed not only by   15
mercantile people, but also by the first noblemen, citizens of every
description, mechanics, seamen, farmers, turf-diggers, chim-
ney-sweeps, footmen, maid-servants, old clothes-women etc. At
first everyone won and no one lost. 'Then, as the gamble grew
wilder, houses and estates were mortgaged. Workmen sold the   20
very tools by which they had gained their livelihood; and some of
the poorest people gained in a few months houses, coaches and
horses, and behaved like the first characters in the land.' One
speculator is said to have made five thousand pounds sterling in
four months, and in a single town, deals to the amount of ten mil-   25
lion pounds were made during the three years the mania lasted.
More often than not, as we have already seen, the bulb never actually changed hands. Let us take an example. A tulip-fancier
would make an engagement with a dealer for a bulb which was to
be delivered and paid for at planting time. If, when autumn came,   30
the bulb had risen in value, the dealer would then pay to the tulip-

fancier the difference between the old and the new price; if it had become cheaper, then the tulip-fancier would pay the difference. In either case the dealer retained the bulb. It was, in short, the familiar gamble of the stock exchange.   35

Suddenly, early in the spring of 1637, the crash came: the amateurs grew bored, and flooded the market; everyone wanted to sell, no one to buy. In vain the unfortunate dealers resorted to such ruses as mock auctions to restore confidence; nobody was deceived. On February 24, delegates from the principal towns of   40 Holland, who met in Amsterdam to discuss what was to be done, agreed that all sales of tulips made before the end of November should be binding. Transactions after that date could be cancelled by the buyer, provided that notice was given before March. But this decision did not satisfy the public. 'When my buyer pays me, I   45 will pay you; but he is nowhere to be found,' says Gaergoedt pathetically. So many lawsuits were filed that the Courts could not deal with them all, and an appeal was made to the magistrates. A petition was sent to the Governors of Holland and West Friesland, urging them to cancel all agreements made during the   50 winter. They replied feebly that they possessed insufficient evidence, and advised the magistrates 'to endeavour to induce the parties to come to terms in a friendly manner'. Soon, however, they were forced to act. In April it was declared by the Court of Holland that every vendor who could not make his purchaser pay   55 might dispose of his bulbs as best he could and claim from him the amount by which the selling price fell short of the original contract. It was also ordered that all contracts should remain in force until further enquiries had been made. Many sellers, however, rather than face delay and uncertainty, preferred to cut their   60 losses and to accept in ready money five or ten per cent of the amount owing to them.

There are many stories, more or less legendary, of the tulipomania. One will suffice. A syndicate of Haarlem florists, hearing that a cobbler at The Hague had succeeded in growing a black   65 tulip, visited him and after some haggling purchased the bulb for fifteen hundred florins. No sooner was it in their possession than they threw it on the ground and trampled it underfoot. 'Idiot!' cried one of them when the astonished cobbler began to protest: 'we have a black tulip too, and chance will never favour you again.   70 We would have given you ten thousand florins if you had asked it.' The wretched cobbler, inconsolable at the thought of the wealth which might have been his, took to his bed and promptly expired.

WILFRID BLUNT, *Tulipomania* (Penguin)

MULTIPLE CHOICE QUESTIONS

After reading each of the following questions, choose the ONE correct answer, and indicate it by writing down the letter that stands for it.

From Section A

1 Paragraph 1 (ll. 1–8) stresses that one variety of Italian tulip grows wild and is native. This type
  A cannot have existed in Europe before 1554
  B surprisingly escaped notice before 1554
  C was represented in some forms of ancient art
  D was included in one genuine Roman mosaic
  E was so common as not to have seemed worth mentioning by Roman authors

2 'Indigenous' (l. 3) means
  A common
  B well-known
  C native
  D formerly cultivated
  E uncomplicated

3 Section A suggests, but does not plainly say, that Busbecq
  A had seen a few tulips before his visit to the Turkish capital
  B first noticed them growing in Turkey rather than in the rest of Europe
  C noticed that they grew wild rather than in gardens
  D found few flowers in the Turkish empire (including Greece) that possessed an attractive smell
  E was sure that the Turks overvalued tulips

4 Which ONE of the following is *not* a fair criticism of the early part of this section?
  A it does not explain why Roman authors ignored a flower that is a native in Italy
  B it uses words such as 'is now generally agreed' which shows that it is not quite certain about some of its statements
  C in ll. 21–2 it does not explain how presents received by an ambassador can *cost* him a lot
  D it does not explain how tulips can flower in the winter
  E it does not make it clear whether the Turks valued the tulip very highly

5 A 'classical author' (l. 1) means
  A someone who wrote in what is now a dead language
  B a Roman or Greek writer living between approximately 600 BC and AD 400
  C someone who writes literature and not books on horticulture

    D a famous author who writes literature of a high quality
    E an informative writer, e.g. a historian

6 Which ONE of the following remarks is *not* true?

    A in the second paragraph the writer is more certain of his facts than he had been in the first
    B the paragraph forming ll. 23–7 consists of a topic sentence, and then four pieces of evidence to prove the first statement
    C ll. 23–44 switch gradually from the topic of tulips' popularity to the topic of their price
    D the writer is shocked by the extravagance of Frenchmen who over-valued rare tulip bulbs
    E ll. 28–44 emphasize the money value of tulips but occasionally imply that they were thought beautiful

7 'Horticulture' (l. 43) means

    A flower-growing
    B painting and similar arts
    C gardening
    D growing crops by means of irrigation
    E the appreciation of beauty

8 Which ONE of the following remarks is *not* true about the high value put on tulips by the French?

    A its development was delayed by the civil wars of religion
    B Section A admits, a little casually, that it amounted to a *craze*
    C Section A stresses how much unhappiness it caused in France
    D it was not quite as extreme in France as it was later to be in Holland
    E it appealed to the middle classes as well as the aristocrats

9 The writer's attitude to the beauty of tulips is to

    A make it a major topic
    B mention it occasionally
    C ignore it
    D make indirect references to it
    E emphasize its appeal to painters

10 In l. 23 which ONE of the following methods of punctuation would *not* be acceptable (instead of a semi-colon)

    A quickly—in 1561
    B quickly: in 1561
    C quickly. In 1561
    D quickly, in 1561
    E quickly . . . . in 1561

From Section B

11 'Tulipomania' means

    A a mad rise in the price of tulip bulbs

B a warm enthusiasm to grow tulips
C the rapid import of tulips into other countries
D the development of new, unusual types of tulip
E a tendency to exaggerate the beauty of tulips

12 The writer makes a pun on two meanings of 'sold' (l. 7): as well as 'exchanged for money', it means

A misled
B led on by enthusiasm
C cheated
D ruined
E baffled

13 'Speculation' (l. 15) means

A foreseeing the future types of tulip to be developed
B actually selling bulbs at a large profit
C buying bulbs and hoping that they would rise in price
D intelligent forecasting of the future
E engaging in a risky business deal

14 'Engagement' (l. 29) means

A pledge
B speculation
C assessment
D guess
E appointment

15 'Ruses' (l. 39) were

A business methods
B desperate dodges
C examples of wishful thinking
D types of cheating
E fraudulent practices

16 'Should be binding' (l. 43) means that they

A could be cancelled by either side
B would be debts of honour, not legally enforceable
C were forecasts of the future likely to come true
D would be accepted as honourable
E would be enforced by the law

17 'Vendor' (l. 55) means

A grower
B speculator
C seller
D trader
E purchaser

18 The attempt to use the Dutch legal system to solve the problems caused by the fall in tulip prices was

  A ineffective
  B half-hearted
  C unpractical
  D unfair
  E premature

19 'Expired' (l. 73) means

  A despaired
  B fell asleep
  C died
  D collapsed
  E gave up hope

20 This writer intends us to consider the story of the black tulip (ll. 64–73) as

  A tragical and depressing
  B different from other stories about tulipomania
  C important evidence of the rich cheating the poor
  D unlikely to be completely accurate
  E very ironical and therefore flippantly amusing

21 The syndicate of Haarlem florists wished to

  A send up the scarcity value of their own black tulip
  B prevent a black tulip from being developed at all
  C make small growers such as the cobbler afraid of their power
  D buy up all rare tulips that came on the market
  E learn how to grow a black tulip

22 'Inconsolable' (l. 72) means that the cobbler could not

  A restrain his anger at having failed to make a fortune
  B be cheered up by the high price he received
  C forgive himself for missing his opportunity
  D be persuaded to develop other new types of tulip
  E be comforted in his distress and depression

TRADITIONAL QUESTIONS

Answer the following questions in your own words as far as possible. Questions marked with an asterisk should be answered *very briefly*, and in these answers complete sentences are not necessary.

From Section A

*1 Give in a single word or short phrase the meaning of *five* of the following words *as used in the passage*:

  i extravagant (l. 20) **ii** spiritual (l. 26) **iii** fantastic (l. 33)
  iv dowry (l. 36) **v** craze (l. 39) **vi** horticulture (l. 43).

2 What do you understand by the expression 'classical author' (l. 1)?

3 Why is 'Roman' (l. 6) in inverted commas?

4 What is the point of the sentence 'I received several presents which cost me not a little' (ll. 21–2)?

5 Explain the expression 'the stage for the most astonishing drama' (ll. 42–3).

From Section B

*6 Give in a single word or short phrase the meaning of *six* of the following words *as used in the passage*:

i sold (l. 7) **ii** outlay (l. 13) **iii** mortgaged (l. 20) **iv** ruses (l. 39)
v delegates (l. 40) **vi** petition (l. 49) **vii** induce (l. 52)
viii syndicate (l. 64).

7 Explain the expressions:
  i 'The tulipomania was at its height' (l. 1)
  ii 'the amateurs grew bored and flooded the market' (ll. 36–7)

8 Explain the following figurative expressions:
  i 'These offsets are the interest, while the capital remains' (ll. 10–11)
  ii 'Hand in hand with tulip-growing went speculation' (ll. 14–15).

9 Why did the tulip dealers arrange mock auctions?

10 What do you understand by the expression 'to cut their losses' (ll. 60–61)?

II. Writing English

Write on ONE of the following:

a Imagine you are moving to a recently built house. You have been given the pleasant task of planning the fairly large garden which surrounds the house. Say how you would set to work, drawing a sketch if you wish. Keep only a small but suitable area for vegetables. Your main job is landscaping, with lawns, rockeries and flowerbeds.
b Country gardens.
c A short story about some flowers of a very unusual kind which have grown from ordinary seeds or bulbs planted in your garden. You plan to show the blooms at a flower show, and have to take steps to protect your garden from possible thieves. Continue with your own ideas.
d   'If a man loses one third of his skin, he dies.
          If a tree loses one third of its bark, it dies.
          If the earth loses one third of its trees, it will die.'
This is the motto of Richard St. Barbe Baker, the founder of the 'Men

of the Trees'. Do you think we are conscious of the need for afforestation and the protection of trees today? Say what you know of this subject, and quote from your own experience in support of your views.

e Timber!

f Write a letter to your local newspaper making out a case for the introduction of by-laws to prevent certain nuisances you have noticed, such as litter, vandalism of any kind, stray dogs, unnecessary noise from houses, works or streets.

g A European country you would like to visit.

h Choose an outdoor occupation, such as gamekeeper, forester, games mistress, farmworker, kennelmaid. Say what appeals to you about such a job, and how you would set about getting it.

Suggestions for Projects, Assignments and Course Work

1 The Himalayan Range—Everest—geography—peoples—attempts, successful and unsuccessful to climb Everest—different routes—the Abominable Snowman.

2 The conquest of disease—medicine and surgery from earliest times to the present day—different problems in different parts of the world—air travel: inoculation and quarantine—the prolonging of life—old age.

3 Roads and travelling—Roman—medieval—18th-century improvements—turnpikes (turnpike riots)—stagecoaches—wayside inns—highwaymen—19th- and 20th-century improvements—the motorcar—the omnibus and charabanc—motorways (return to turnpike or tollgate system).

III. Using English

Revise uses of the dash (interruptions of a sentence or speech; before an explanation; one before and after a parenthesis, like brackets).

N.B. a row of dots . . . indicates an unfinished sentence or remark, but not by reason of interruption (for which a dash is used).

Punctuation

1 Account for the following marks of punctuation in the passage in Part I:
   i the semi-colons in paragraph 1 of Section A   **ii** the commas after 'Busbecq' (l.A. 9) and after 'Magnificent' (l.A. 10)   **iii** the semi-colon after 'it' (l.A. 17)   **iv** the commas after 'France' (l.A. 28) and after 'gardening' (l.A. 29)   **v** the inverted commas before and after 'Mère brune' (l.A. 34)   **vi** the brackets before 'where' (l.A. 40) and after 'garden' (l.A. 42)   **vii** the colon after '1623' (l.B. 5)   **viii** the semi-colon after 'tulips' (l.B. 13)   **ix** the commas after 'Then' (l.B. 19) and after 'wilder' (l.B. 20)   **x** the commas before and after 'in short' (l.B. 34)   **xi** the colon after 'came' (l.B. 36)   **xii** the inverted commas before 'to' (l.B. 52) and after 'manner' (l.B. 53).

2 Construct sentences to show one use each of the colon and semi-colon, and two uses of inverted commas (four sentences in all).

Grammar and Usage

3 For each of the following words (all used in ll.A. 1–23 of the passage in Part I) give the corresponding part of speech as indicated (e.g. confidence—verb: confide):

i probability—adjective   **ii** identified—verb   **iii** varieties—verb
iv grow—noun   **v** uncommon—adverb   **vi** abundance—verb
vii our—pronoun   **viii** season—adjective   **ix** strong—noun
x extravagant—noun   **xi** cost—adjective   **xii** fame—adjective.

4 Say what is wrong with the following sentences. Write a correct version of each, making as little alteration as possible:

i He repeated his protest twice all over again.   **ii** Scrambling up the hillside, the view became more beautiful.   **iii** The policeman affected an entry through the medium of the side door.   **iv** The hills in Shropshire are as high, if not higher, than the Yorkshire wolds.   **v** Of the two books I read last week, this one is the best.

Spelling and Dictionary Work

5 The following words are incomplete. The dots indicate a letter or letters missing. The number of the dots bears no relationship to the number of letters missing. Write down the words, spelling them correctly.

i a . . . . . uire (gain)   **ii** s . . . . . ze (grasp)   **iii** su . . . . . rise
(astonish)   **iv** immediat . . . . . ly   **v** misch . . . . . ous (playfully
annoying)   **vi** g . . . . . ge (measure)   **vii** embar . . . . . sed
viii cent . . . . . ry (100).

6 Use the following words in separate sentences so as to bring out the differences in meaning:

i intimidate, discourage, terrorize   **ii** drowsy, tired, exhausted
iii instruction, tuition, education.

Style and Appreciation

7 Read the following description of the Sussex Downs by Alan Ross and show how he makes his description vivid.

Under this laundered blueness of September, the fresh clumps on the Downs stand out in their singed colours, altering daily, as clear as birthmarks. It has been a month of sunsets, flat bars of flamingo and cobalt and gold softening behind squat, Downland churches, and the windmills, darkening in their arrested semaphore along the spine of these whale-like hills, barriers to the sea and the south-westerlies. Tractors and cars crunch in fading light up these dusty lanes, marched first by legionaries; and driving sometimes at dusk over the Beacon into Brighton, one passes cattle lowing in the mist round the old dew ponds.

ALAN ROSS, *Cape Summer and the Australians in England* (Curtis Brown)

Pay particular attention to imagery, the use of colour and sound. [Refer to Unit I, Part III (6)]

Books to read

The Bafut Beagles	Gerald Durrell
Man Meets Dog	Konrad Lorenz
Short Stories	Paul Gallico
Animal Farm	George Orwell
Sherlock Holmes stories	A. Conan Doyle
The Ship	C. S. Forester
Quest in Paradise	David Attenborough
A Sort of Traitors	Nigel Balchin
The Once and Future King	T. H. White

Unit 7

I. Reading and Understanding

I. Reading and Understanding

Read the following passage (which for your convenience has been divided into four sections) and then answer the questions.

THE HISTORY OF ADVERTISING

[A]   Advertising is as old as Humanity: indeed, much older; for what are the flaunting colours of the flowers but so many invitations to the bees to come and 'buy our product'? Everything is already there: the striking forms, the brilliant hues, even the 'conditioning of the customer'. One can almost see 'personal shoppers 5 only' inscribed at the entrance to the flower. But in human terms, advertising might be defined as any device which first arrests the attention of the passer-by and then induces him to accept a mutually advantageous exchange.

In its most primitive form advertising is merely an an- 10 nouncement that somebody has something to sell: a bush outside the hut of a wine-seller, or an inscription in chalk or charcoal beside the door of Greek theatre or Roman circus. When paper came into use the inscription would be written on that, and affixed to wall or post—which, incidentally, is the original meaning of the 15 word 'poster'; something stuck on a post.

Lettered posters, of course, imply the existence of a literate public. When this was lacking, as in the Middle Ages, the poster gave place to the crier. Posters did not appear again until the end of the fifteenth century and they seem to have been used at first for 20 political purposes. With the invention of printing they proliferated and governments were compelled to enact stringent laws to govern their use. Official posters, for example royal proclamations, were the first to use pictures, usually merely the royal arms. Recruiting posters were embellished with woodcuts, sometimes 25 coloured by hand and, in the early years of the eighteenth century, troupes of acrobats began to make use of the same device.

Woodcut was, by its nature, somewhat crude in its technique, and it was a great advance when, in the early nineteenth century, the process of lithography was discovered. The true pictorial 30 poster was now possible but it remained obstinately monochrome until half way through the century. Then, in England, experiments began to be made of printing lithographs from several stones, a different coloured ink being used on each. The results were used to advertise the melodramas so popular at the period. The drawing   35 was crudely realistic and the colours blatant but technically such posters marked a real advance.

[B] Meanwhile advertising had spread to other media of communication: the newspapers and magazines. Even in the eighteenth century newspapers had carried rather timid little announcements of goods for sale. What transformed the situation was the rise of pictorial journalism in the 1840s. Most of the illus-   5 trations were in woodcut, or rather wood-engraving, for the level of craftsmanship had risen sharply with the use of small squares of hard box-wood screwed together. A fine line was now possible, and indeed some of the blocks in a magazine like *The Illustrated London News* are miracles of technical skill.   10

Advertisers, however, were still fumbling in the dark. Some of them thought that mere repetition was enough, and that it helped to sell their product if they simply printed its name over and over again on the same page. Repetition is, of course, a very important element in advertising but not, perhaps, in this primitive form. A   15 mere announcement, however often repeated, is not enough. It is necessary to catch the eye and this can most easily be done by some striking image, coupled if possible with an arresting slogan: a monkey in evening dress holding up a shining immaculate frying pan, and, in large letters over his head: 'Monkey Brand Won't   20 Wash Clothes'. This 'negative approach' is still a potent weapon in the advertiser's armoury.

We can trace the beginnings of a more penetrating psychology in the 'Before and After' advertisements so popular in the last quarter of the nineteenth century: a picture of a wretched creature   25 who has not yet taken *our* pill, and the same transformed into heroic manhood after he had taken it; or a picture of a woman on the left with long, lank hair who has not yet tumbled to the fact that with the aid of *our* curlers she can transform herself into the kind of professional beauty depicted on the right.   30

Snob-appeal was already beginning to raise its enticing head, and some of it was of a blatancy which would hardly be permitted today. In the 1870s tailors' advertisements almost invariably showed the head of some prominent politician, or even of some Royal Personage, stuck on the top of a tailor's dummy. Did they   35 mind? We have no record of any prosecution. Was Mr Gladstone distressed when he was depicted as chopping down trees while wearing an Electropathic Belt? And what of the advertisement which shows him presiding over a Cabinet meeting with every member of the Cabinet named, and all singing the praises of one particular brand of tea?   40

[C]   In the technological sphere all kinds of novelties were being introduced: the 'penny-farthing' and, later, the 'safety' bicycle; the primitive motor-car; a waterproof 'free from odour' (the earlier oilskins stank like a pole-cat); the first refrigerator, called a 'self-feeding Ice Safe', making it unnecessary to buy 'Original   5 Blocks of ice from High Lakes, Christiania, Norway' at 7/6d per cwt; primitive roller-skates; revolving heels ('the Most Useful Invention of the Victorian Era'), and a phonograph 'Loud as a Man Sings'.

Another striking change is in the accepted ideal of feminine   10 beauty. There are few slimming advertisements but we find plenty informing us that Cadbury's Cocoa is composed of 'Flesh Forming Ingredients', or recommending various methods of increasing the size of the bust. Flat-chestedness was indeed regarded as one of the greatest possible misfortunes. What we would now consider   15 as a very well-formed girl is shown as utterly neglected while all the gentlemen pay court to a prima donna-like lady with a bosom like the figure-head of a ship.

[D]   And of course the advertisements themselves have improved—if improvement it be. What strikes us about Victorian publicity is its comparative naivety—its lack of psychological understanding. Freud had hardly yet been heard of, and no-one had tumbled to the idea that 'sex will sell anything'. Our advertisers have become much cleverer: in fact, as some might think,   5 too clever by half. Chesterton, more than a generation ago, was pointing out the dangerous element in the new techniques and, since his day, the power of advertising has increased a hundredfold. The Devil's progress would seem to be: Advertiser—Public   10 Relations Officer—Minister of Propaganda—Big Brother.

Propaganda indeed is the new Magic. It does not operate on the plane of the conscious intelligence. No-one was ever converted by its arguments; in fact it hardly proceeds by arguments at all. It deals in affirmations, repeated until their effect is hypnotic. It   15 deals in suggestions aimed at the weakest link in the victims' armour; and the weakest link is where the conscious and the unconscious join. A slogan is a spell of words; a party badge or a trade symbol, a magical emblem.

LEONARD DE VRIES, *Victorian Advertisements* (John Murray)

MULTIPLE CHOICE QUESTIONS

After reading each of the following questions, choose the ONE correct answer, and indicate it by writing down the letter that stands for it.

From Section A

1 'Flaunting' (l. 2) means

    A inviting
    B showy
    C bright
    D sensational
    E attractive

2 In ll. 7–10 the passage defines the two components of advertisement. Which ONE of the following remarks is *not* true about them?

    A as far as bees are concerned flowers illustrate both the first and the second
    B primitive forms of making announcements served both of these purposes
    C recruiting posters illustrated the second but not the first
    D in discussing coloured posters Section A is more aware of the first than of the second
    E in general, Section A says very little about the second

3 'Primitive' (l. 10) means

    A original
    B traditional
    C antiquated
    D simple
    E out-of-date

4 'Proliferated' (l. 21) means that they became more

    A attractive
    B sophisticated
    C outspoken
    D daring
    E numerous

5 'Stringent' (l. 22) means

    A puritanical
    B vindictive
    C strict
    D oppressive
    E clear

6 This writer is not very critical of advertisements as distinct from propaganda. One of his few criticisms of advertising is that

    A advertising was invented long ago

B the exchanges of goods produced by advertising are 'mutually advantageous' (l. 9)

C the Greeks and Romans used it

D governments used pictorial posters

E the drawings on certain advertisements were 'crudely realistic' (l. 36)

From Section B

7 A decisive step in the history of advertisements occurred when

A they first spread to newspapers and magazines

B eighteenth-century newspapers announced what goods were for sale

C in the 1840s newspapers developed modern types of journalism

D in the 1840s newspapers began to print pictures

E the printers of magazines like the *Illustrated London News* developed greater technical skill

8 'Transformed' (l. 4) means

A changed

B modified

C reversed

D revolutionized

E modernized

9 Which ONE of the following is *not* a metaphor?

A 'the level of craftsmanship has risen sharply' (ll. 6–7)

B 'Advertisers were still fumbling in the dark' (l. 11)

C 'the beginnings of a more penetrating psychology' (l. 23)

D 'Snob-appeal was already beginning to raise its enticing head' (l. 31)

E 'of a blatancy which would hardly be permitted today' (l. 32)

10 In an advertisement, repetition

A needs to be subtly hidden

B helps to sell things

C needs reinforcing by a striking picture

D must appeal to the reader's eye

E depends upon the slogan that accompanies it

11 An advertisement that says what the product will *not* do will probably

A rely too much on repetition

B turn out to be too negative

C appeal too strongly to our sense of humour

D confuse its readers

E influence its readers effectively

12 Advertisers were still 'fumbling in the dark' (l. 11) means that they

    A were handicapped by being unable to use colours

    B had no real knowledge of how advertising methods could be improved

    C placed too naîve a trust in the effect of repetition

    D had not learnt how to light up posters

    E were using too primitive methods of reproducing colour

13 The author regards the Monkey Brand advertisement (ll. 20–21) as

    A witty because it does not repeat itself

    B ineffective because it tells the customer what not to do

    C striking because its words and picture achieve surprise

    D different from previous ones because it includes an animal

    E an example of the effectiveness of self-confident assertion

14 The author regards the 'Before and After' type of advertisements as

    A producing too extravagant a view of how consumers could be changed

    B an old-fashioned type of advertisement now out-of-date

    C illustrating changes that were true as well as surprising

    D containing some informative element

    E depending for its success on its snob-appeal

15 'Tumbled to the fact' (l. 28) is slightly ironic because it

    A states the opposite of what was really true

    B treats as a sober *fact* something that is untrue or at least exaggerated

    C tends to contradict itself

    D suggests that the woman in the advertisement was too trusting

    E suggests that she is like someone who slips

16 The last paragraph (ll. 31–41) emphasises that Victorian advertisers

    A used methods that would lead to prosecutions today

    B manipulated their readers' feeling of social inferiority

    C appealed to their readers' sense of humour

    D used some of the techniques of the political cartoonist

    E developed a deliberate sense of incongruity

17 'Blatancy' (l. 32) means

    A vulgar display

    B confidence showmanship

    C showy vulgarity

    D shameless obviousness

    E barefaced cheek

From Section C

18 The main purpose of including the first paragraph of Section C is that it

A lists new inventions which have to be advertised to sell
B makes all Victorian inventions seem comic
C stresses how advertisements have changed
D gives important examples of how applied science was changing civilization
E deals with inventions for men before the next paragraph deals with inventions for women

19 Victorian advertisements suggest that a slim girl was considered

A unattractive
B unhealthy
C fashionable
D popular
E undernourished

From Section D

20 'Naivety' (l. 3) means

A subtlety
B truthfulness
C repetitiveness
D cleverness
E simplicity

21 In the sentence in ll. 10–11, 'Big Brother' refers to Orwell's novel *1984*: it means that advertisements

A have become more sophisiticated in their techniques
B make an increasing use of sex appeal
C have produced techniques that might be used by a totalitarian government
D have converted consumers by being genuinely informative
E make clever use of their readers' subconscious impulses

22 This article calls propaganda 'the new Magic' (l. 12) because it

A makes use of people's superstition
B uses words that have subconscious effects
C employs rather obvious methods
D avoids repetition of the same idea
E argues that advertisement has partly replaced religion

23 Which ONE of the following words or phrases does *not* stress the danger involved in advertising?

A 'too clever by half' (l. 7)
B 'dangerous element' (l. 8)
C 'the power of advertising' (l. 9)
D 'the Devil's progress' (l. 10)
E 'conscious intelligence' (l. 13)

TRADITIONAL QUESTIONS

Answer the following questions in your own words as far as possible. Questions marked with an asterisk should be answered *very briefly*, and in these answers complete sentences are not necessary.

From Section A

*1 Give in a single word or short phrase the meaning of *four* of the following words *as used in the passage*:

i flaunting (l. 2) ii striking (l. 4) iii arrests (l. 7)
iv proliferated (l. 21) v stringent (l. 22) vi embellished (l. 25)
vii blatant (l. 36).

2 With what are the flowers and the bees compared in paragraph 1?

3 Put into your own words the first sentence of paragraph 3 (ll. 17–18).

4 Why did posters disappear in favour of a town crier?

5 Deduce from the context what 'the process of lithography' (l. 30) was.

6 Explain the expression 'it remained obstinately monochrome' (l. 31).

From Section B

*7 Give in a single word or short phrase the meaning of *five* of the following words *as used in the passage*:

i media (l. 1) ii timid (l. 3) iii immaculate (l. 19) iv potent (l. 21)
v lank (l. 28) vi enticing (l. 31).

8 What was the reason for the appearance on a large scale of advertisements in newspapers and magazines?

9 What is meant by the sentence 'Advertisers were still fumbling in the dark' (l. 11)?

10 Why is repetition in advertising not sufficient in itself?

11 How does the 'negative approach' (l. 21) differ from the 'Before and After' (l. 24) in advertising?

12 Explain the expression 'Snob-appeal' (l. 31).

From Section C

*13 Give in a single word or short phrase the meaning of the following words *as used in the passage*:

i technological (l. 1) ii novelties (l. 1) iii primitive (l. 3)
iv accepted (l. 10).

14 In paragraph 1, what were the 'novelties' advertised mainly concerned with?

15 There are two comparisons in this section: i 'the earlier oilskins stank *like a pole-cat*' (ll. 3–4) and ii 'a lady with a bosom *like the figurehead of a ship*' (ll. 17–18). Would you regard either or both of these as similes? Give your reasons.

From Section D

*16 Give in a single word or short phrase the meaning of *three* of the following words *as used in the passage*:
   i naivety (l. 3)   ii tumbled (l. 5)   iii techniques (l. 8)
   iv converted (l. 13).

17 Why does the writer add the afterthought '—if improvement it be' (l. 2)?

18 What is the meaning of 'too clever by half' (l. 7)?

19 What is the point of the last sentence of paragraph 1?

20 With what are the buying public compared in paragraph 2?

21 Show how the idea of propaganda being magic (l. 12) is repeated later in the same paragraph.

22 Explain the expression 'It deals in suggestions aimed at the weakest link in the victims' armour' (ll. 15–17).

From the whole passage

23 Suggest titles for each Section.

24 Summarize the whole passage in about 200 of your own words.

II. Writing English

Write on ONE of the following:

a 'Do advertisements make our lives nastier or nicer?' (Marghanita Laski).
b Write a story telling how you bought a product which you had seen advertised. Tell how the results were very different from what you had been promised.
c Market-day.
d In what ways are newspapers useful and necessary to us?
e Silence is golden.
f On failing examinations.

g Has our age mistaken comfort for civilization?

h 'I awoke one morning and found myself famous.'

i Write a story, a description or an essay suggested by the illustration. (Your composition may be directly about the subject of the illustration, or may only take suggestions from it, but there must be some clear connection between the illustration and the composition.)

Suggestions for Projects, Assignments and Coursework.

1 Make an analysis of your local newspaper. Calculate the space given (column inches) to the different components of the paper, e.g. national news, local news, letters, advertisements, photographs, cartoons, reviews of books and films etc. The relative importance of these might be shown by constructing a table or histogram. What service does the paper give? What power has it over local affairs?

2 Your own poetry anthology. Include about ten poems you have read and found interesting and/or memorable. Discuss two or three of these in detail. Show clearly what appeals to you in each of these poems, remembering that you should write about both style and content. Give a reason for including each one of the poems in your anthology. Why not try adding a poem of your own composition?

*'I hate to keep raising the
prices each week but they've
come to expect it.'*

3 Superstitions—origins—in different parts of the world—connexion with religion, pagan and Christian—prophecies and coincidences—omens.

III. Using English

Punctuation

Revise uses of the apostrophe (letter or letters omitted; possession—beware singular and plural)

If you are doubtful about a word ending in 's', try turning the expression into an 'of' phrase. When this cannot be done there is no need for an apostrophe. For example:

'A row of potatoes.' Do you need an apostrophe? Turn into an 'of' phrase. This gives you 'potatoes of a row'. Compare this with 'the dogs bone' which becomes 'the bone of the dog'. An apostrophe is needed. To determine where to put the apostrophe, follow this plan:

i Turn your expression into an 'of' phrase: 'the dogs bone' becomes 'the bone of the *dog*'.

ii To the word *dog* in your 'of' phrase add 's, thus giving you *dog's*.

iii Was the word *dog* in your 'of' phrase a plural ending in 's'?
If the answer is no (as here) leave *dog's* as in **ii**.
If the answer is yes you would then strike off the final 's' in **ii**.

Examples: 'the twins dolls'—'the dolls of the *twins*'—add 's to *twins*—*twins's*—was *twins* a plural ending in 's'?—yes—strike off final 's', leaving *twins'*, 'the childrens books'—'the books of the *children*'—add 's—*children's*—was *children* a plural ending in 's'—no—leave the word as *children's*.

N.B. His, hers, theirs, ours, yours, whose, its (as a possessive).
Beware of it's (it is), theirs and there's (there is).

1 Account for the following marks of punctuation used in the passage in Part I:

i the colon after 'there' (l.A. 4) **ii** the commas before and after 'of course' (l.A. 17) **iii** the inverted commas before and after 'Before and After' (l.B. 24) **iv** the inverted commas before 'Loud' (l.C. 8) and after 'Sings' (l.C. 9) **v** the dashes after 'Advertiser' (l.D. 10), 'Public Relations Officer' (l.D. 10) and 'Minister of Propaganda' (l.D. 11) **vi** the capital M in 'Magic' (l.D. 12).

2 Rewrite the following in more connected form with correct punctuation:

You should keep dogs—fine animals—sagacious creatures—dog of my own once—Pointer—surprising instinct—out shooting one day—entering enclosure—whistled—dog stopped—whistled again—Ponto—no go—stock still—called him—Ponto, Ponto—wouldn't move—dog transfixed—staring at a board—looked up, saw an inscription—'Gamekeeper has orders to shoot all dogs found in this enclosure'—wouldn't pass it—wonderful dog—valuable dog that—very.

Grammar and Usage

3 Show that the following words have two different meanings by including them in sentences (two for each word):

i strike **ii** catch **iii** form **iv** post **v** size **vi** court **vii** deal **viii** spell.

4 Correct the following sentences where necessary, giving reasons for the corrections you make:

i It will be left to you or I to make a decision. **ii** I will drown and nobody shall save me. **iii** It is almost unique for a week to go by without a strike in some industry. **iv** Persons not putting waste paper in this basket will be punished. **v** He literally hung on to the edge of the cliff by his finger nails. **vi** All too often adult's write unsuitable childrens' books.

Spelling and Dictionary Work

5 The following words are incomplete. The dots indicate a letter or letters missing. The number of dots bears no relationship to the number of letters missing. Rewrite the words spelling them correctly.

i com...t...ee **ii** ch...f (leader) **iii** med...cine
iv el...g...ble (suitable) **v** dec...tfu...(misleading)
vi simil...r **vii** Ar...ic (of the north pole) **viii** fo...ty (40)
ix criti...ism **x** for...ell (prophesy).

6 Use a dictionary to find out the derivation of the following words:

i ponder **ii** liquorice **iii** chump **iv** sonnet **v** waltz
vi bawbee **vii** bayonet **viii** trumpery.

Style and Appreciation

7 Use *five* of the following words in sentences as metaphors:

i comb **ii** furrow **iii** shepherd **iv** paint **v** peak **vi** string
vii fence **viii** blanket.

8   *Esther's Tomcat*

Daylong this tomcat lies stretched flat
As an old rough mat, no mouth and no eyes.
Continual wars and wives are what
Have tattered his ears and battered his head.

Like a bundle of old rope and iron
Sleeps till blue dusk. Then reappear
His eyes, green as ringstones: he yawns wide red,
Fangs fine as a lady's needle and bright.

A tomcat sprang at a mounted knight,
Locked round his neck like a trap of hooks
While the knight rode fighting its clawing and bite.
After hundreds of years the stain's there

On the stone where he fell, dead of the tom:
That was at Barnborough. The tomcat still
Grallochs odd dogs on the quiet,
Will take the head clean off your simple pullet,

Is unkillable. From the dog's fury,
From gunshot fired point-blank he brings
His skin whole, and whole
From owlish moons of bekittenings

Among ashcans. He leaps and lightly
Walks upon sleep, his mind on the moon.
Nightly over the round world of men,
Over the roofs go his eyes and outcry.

TED HUGHES, Lupercal (Faber and Faber)

Read the remarks about Poetry on pages 191–2 and then write an appreciation of the poem 'Esther's Tomcat'. The title does not indicate anything
about the poet's viewpoint, attitude or purpose; in other words, the title
does not indicate the theme, which deals mainly with the toughness and
ferocity of the cat. Always try to state the theme of any poem you are appreciating.

Books to read

The Pit Mouth	H. M. Tomlinson
This Great Journey	Jennie Lee
Scoop	Evelyn Waugh
The Chrysalids	John Wyndham
Tarka the Otter	Henry Williamson
One Pair of Hands	Monica Dickens
Aspects of Science Fiction	ed. G. D. Doherty
Fair Stood the Wind for France	H. E. Bates
Greenmantle	John Buchan

Unit 8

I. Reading and Understanding

Read the following passage (which for your convenience has been divided into three sections) and then answer the questions.

VICTORIAN SEA-FRONTS

[A]   Noise and uproar is what strikes one most when one tries to recapture the atmosphere of Victorian sea-fronts, and the din was a constant complaint of contemporaries. The ground-bass was provided, from end to end of Victoria's reign, by the itinerant band—cornets, clarinets, horns and trombones, usually out of   5
tune—the German band, which was to be found, it seems, at almost every street corner. It added to the pandemonium of the 'front', for the noises are greatly increased in volume and variety as one gets on to the teeming beach itself. Here, actively or potentially vociferous, could be found: children, happy or in   10
tears; dogs; donkeys; goat chaises; sellers of brandyballs, boats, children's socks, lug worms, lace collars, shell-work boxes, jet objects from Whitby; vendors of glass tumblers with hearty inscriptions such as 'Good old Mother-in-Law' or 'Aunt Julia's Half-Pint'; women with trays of imitation jewellery; old women   15
hawking indigestible cakes; 'artists', guaranteeing a pleasing likeness for sixpence, frame included; harp and accordion bands; comb and paper bands; organ grinders, in cosmopolitan uniforms and often drunk, with monkeys; foreigners, wearing sheepskins and leg bandages, with bagpipes and penny whistles; dirty and   20
blasphemous foreigners with a wiry piano on a truck; very dirty foreign boys selling broken-hearted guinea-pigs; 'professors' in black velvet spangled tights; Punch and Judy shows with risqué dialogue and depressed Tobies; music-hall singers; Highland pipers from the glens of Shoreditch   25

[B]   And, amid all the other dins, the hall-mark of the period, the 'negro melodists', 'Uncle Bones and His Men' or whatever they might be called, with banjo, bones and concertina, dressed in coloured tail-coats with bright lapels and large satin buttons, satin waistcoats and gay, striped trousers, frilled shirts with high   5
striped Gladstone collars and huge spotted bow-ties, striped

socks, gloves, pumps on their feet and on their heads either miniature top hats in bright colours or straw hats with striped ribbons.
All through the period, from the 'fifties onwards, the nigger minstrels sang their songs on the beaches and piers, sometimes planta- 10
tion songs (*I wish I were in Old Virginny*) but more often the
popular ballads and music-hall ditties of the year, singing with
great variety anything from *The Death of Nelson* in the same programme with *The Beautiful Spring Onion* or *I Can't Stand Mrs
Green's Mother*, and singing the refrains always with much 15
expression and verve:

> Oh, what dear little hinnercent Things they har!
> They're Hangels without any wings, they har!
> Oh, my love is so 'ot 20
> I could kiss all the lot,
> The dear little Hinnercent Things!

They had a long innings, starting in the 'fifties with a stream of
touring troupes from America and continuing to just before the 25
turn of the century when, quite suddenly, the Mohawk Minstrels and all the rest of them faded away, and blackened faces
and spotted bows were replaced by whitened faces and pom-
poms, by the Clifford Essex team, Adeler and Sutton's and
countless others, until in 1900 the *Daily News* could state finally 30
that 'niggers at the seaside have given place to pierrots', and that
minstrelsy had closed down. But that horrible institution, the
Weekly Singing Competition, ('Now then, which is the little gal to
step out first and get a medal?') was handed on, unchanged, from
one to the other. 35

[C] But there were two other features of the seaside in general,
two exclusive fruits of our island genius, which were common to
the uninhibited vacations of the coster and to the holidays of a
large proportion of the Victorian middle class. They were both
survivals of the eighteenth century and both apparently immuta- 5
ble—the seaside lodging-house, and the bathing machine.
   The exorbitance and opportunism of seaside landladies was
already a sore point in 1780. As the nineteenth century progresses
this tradition of frugality in the lodging- or boarding-house is sup-
plemented by less worthy qualities. Dirt, for one. It is interesting 10
that a small boy, obviously of comfortable middle-class parents,
should be depicted in an illustrated joke of 1857 as exclaiming, as
he displays a crab he has found on the beach, 'Oh, look here,
mama! I've caught a fish just like those thingamies in my bed at

our lodgings!'; and bugs, together with the defective drainage, be-   15
came a common complaint. Another was dependent upon the fact
that one still bought locally, or imported from town, one's own
provisions. This led, it was claimed, to a constant winnowing
away, behind the scenes, of one's tea and sugar, and drink in particular, by the landlady, to whom embittered widowhood and a   20
partiality for brandy are invariably attributed. Her numerous
grandchildren, apt to have either whooping-cough or a piano,
were a further cause of offence.

The decoration of her rooms, to the contemplation of which
wet days so often condemned one, was by the 'seventies set in a   25
mould that was to persist to the present time. We read even then of
the hypnotizing pattern of the wallpaper, of the mustachioed portrait of her late husband, and of herself before her constitution
had been ruined by her lodgers' brandy, of the dusty, fringed cur-
tains and the grate filled with tawdry tomfoolery in the way of   30
fancy paper and shavings.

An additional worry to the well-to-do Victorian housewife on
holiday was the constant dread of what might be happening in her
own home in town. For it was the custom then to import, during
one's absence, some 'respectable woman' as caretaker, who was   35
again likely to be given to 'brown brandy in her tea,' to abuse her
position and introduce into one's home a number of male topers
to batten on the modest but ample cellar then kept in the house.

The second universal feature of the seaside, the bathing
machine, still maintained, though in infinitely greater numbers,   40
exactly the same form as when it was first introduced. The cost of
hiring it remained more or less constant: from a shilling at
Brighton and sixpence at Scarborough during the Regency
—exclusive of 'perquisites', which included a tip to the attendants, usually equal to the cost of hiring—it seems to have been   45
levelled down to ninepence a time pretty well anywhere during
Victoria's reign, with reductions for series of tickets and for children. There were still queues for the machines, though the sea
might be obscured from the beach by a solid fringe of them.

But although it multiplied in numbers the bathing machine   50
went down in popular esteem and by the 'seventies had become an
object of ridicule, an amusing,' but uncomfortable and at times
dangerous, relic. People complained of its abrasive, pebble-
strewn floor, the smell of old seaweed, the pinless pincushions and
broken bootjacks—but still more of the behaviour of the drivers,   55
who would rap peremptorily on the door with a shout of 'Right!',
start with a jerk and bounce you about like a ball. Sometimes they
kept you imprisoned long after you were ready to come ashore,

sometimes they trundled you out before you were half dressed, in
which case you experienced for five minutes all the annoyance of   60
dressing in a high wind at sea. Moreover the thing was clumsy and
grotesque: 'It seems rather absurd,' writes a contributor to the
Graphic in 1871, 'to employ a man, a horse and a great house on
wheels to enable a British human creature to dip himself in the
sea.'   65

Both as regards safety and decency English bathing was very
unfavourably compared with the Continental; and as more and
more English people went abroad for their holidays, bringing
back news of the safe and convenient arrangements of bathing
huts, wooden pathways over the shingle and safety ropes in the   70
sea, it became clear that a change would have to be made. It took a
long time to bring about, but as the century drew to a close the
bathing machine was stripped of certain of its trappings to accord
with the alteration, under foreign influence, of English beach
habits.   75

The canopy at the back was the first to disappear, though this
survived well into the 'nineties. The bathing woman faded away at
about the same time. The horse was the next to go, and the bathing
man who looked after it. A few lingered on up to the outbreak of
the war of 1914, but in general the bathing machines, or vans, as 80
they had now sometimes come to be called, became static, lined up
at first at high-water mark and then a few years later withdrawn to
the back of the beach. There they were gradually replaced, from
about 1908 onwards, first by inconvenient and unstable tents and
then by lines of wheelless, semi-permanent huts, such as one finds 85
in most English resorts to-day.

CHRISTOPHER MARSDEN, *The English at the Seaside* (Collins)

MULTIPLE CHOICE QUESTIONS

After reading each of the following questions, choose the ONE correct
answer, and indicate it by writing down the letter that stands for it.

From Section A

1 All the following words contribute to the impression of noisiness
EXCEPT
A 'uproar' (l. 1)
B 'ground-bass' (l. 3)
C 'pandemonium' (l. 7)
D 'vociferous' (l. 10)
E 'cosmopolitan' (l. 18)

2 The writer ought perhaps to have stressed more consistently that all the people in his long list make a noise. One example of people whose noisiness he has omitted to stress is:

    A 'children . . . in tears' (ll. 10–11)
    B 'old women hawking cakes' (ll. 15–16)
    C 'foreigners with bagpipes and penny-whistles' (ll. 19–20)
    D 'blasphemous foreigners' (l. 21)
    E '"professors" in black velvet tights' (ll. 22–3)

3 The mention of 'Highland pipers from the glens of Shoreditch' introduces an element of

    A history
    B romance
    C culture
    D pretence
    E noisiness

4 The contemporaries in l. 3 were people who were

    A rather sensitive to noise
    B describing what they saw
    C living in Victorian times
    D merely visiting the seaside
    E trying to improve conditions

5 Each of the following adds to the humour EXCEPT

    A suggesting that the German band was out of tune (l. 5)
    B stressing that the volume of noise grew as one got nearer to the beach (ll. 8–9)
    C using the word 'guaranteeing' in l. 16 to suggest that the artists exaggerated
    D repeating 'foreigners' in ll. 19 and 21, and repeating 'dirty' in ll. 20 and 21.
    E suggesting that the Punch and Judy show included risqué dialogue (ll. 23–4)

6 Which ONE of the following remarks about the punctuation is *not* correct?

    A In ll. 5 and 6 the dashes mark off an afterthought inserted to describe the band
    B In l. 10 the colon introduces a long list of people who make various noises
    C Each semi-colon in ll. 11–24 ends an item in the list
    D the use of a comma after 'brandyballs' (l. 11) etc indicates that 'sellers . . . . . Whitby' is thought of as one whole item in the long list
    E the inverted commas round 'artists' indicate the writer's genuine respect for their competence

From Section B

7 Which ONE of the following is closest in meaning to 'hall-mark' as used in l. 1?

A proof of genuineness
B distinctive feature
C indication of standard
D representative symbol
E fashionable catchword

8 Of the songs that the nigger minstrels sang, those that concerned America's Deep South formed

A none of them
B very few of them
C a large proportion of them
D most of them
E all of them

9 The nigger-minstrels sang their songs

A enthusiastically
B insincerely
C conventionally
D untunefully
E melodramatically

10 Which ONE of the following statements about nigger minstrels best summarizes the paragraph forming ll. 1–35?

A they attracted large audiences from the beginning of the Victorian age till after 1900
B they were popular from about 1850 to just before 1900
C they were as noisy as the other entertainers who flocked to the Victorian seaside
D they were the most ridiculously dressed of all the Victorian entertainers
E they encouraged their listeners to take part in weekly singing competitions

From Section C

11 Section C stresses those aspects of the Victorian seaside that were

A rarely criticized during that time
B newly developed during the nineteenth century
C completely unknown in other countries
D comparatively expensive and commercialized
E almost completely similar to the modern seaside

12 The use of the word 'uninhibited' (l. 3) suggests that the costers on holiday

A stayed at each seaside resort for only a few days

    B enjoyed themselves naturally without worrying about codes of behaviour
    C had uneducated and unintelligent ideas of pleasure
    D were able to leave their work for only a short time
    E spent extravagantly money that they had saved with difficulty

13 Which ONE of the following is closest in meaning to 'immutable' as used in l. 5?

    A traditional
    B unmatchable
    C unparallelled
    D unchangeable
    E laughable

14 Seaside landladies

    A were conventional in their behaviour
    B seized every opportunity to overcharge
    C neglected hygiene and normal commercial practice
    D were eager to talk openly about their private misfortunes
    E often embarrassed their guests and intruded on their privacy

15 Lines 18–23 suggest that the typical landlady

    A allowed her grandchildren to do what they liked
    B could be proved to have been too fond of alcohol
    C gradually stole her guests' own food and drink
    D underfed her boarders and allowed them very little alcohol
    E knew how to separate the better food from the cheaper

16 The typical landlady's grandchildren

    A insulted the guests
    B stole the guests' food
    C passed on diseases to the guests
    D annoyed the guests
    E amused the guests

17 The phrase 'respectable woman' in l. 35 is printed with inverted commas to show that

    A the phrase is intended to be emphasized
    B the phrase expresses the writer's own opinion
    C the woman was often less respectable than she claimed to be
    D the article is quoting the exact words of a famous Victorian writer
    E Victorian employers were contemptuous of their servants

18 The paragraph that forms ll. 39–49 stresses that bathing machines

    A became more of an expensive luxury
    B did not become much more numerous
    C were not as safe as they seemed

   D changed their design very little

   E were made virtually compulsory by Victorian prudery

19 The next paragraph (ll. 50–65) stresses the bathing machine's

   A popularity

   B large numbers

   C ridiculousness

   D disadvantages

   E lack of comfort

20 Which ONE of the following statements about English bathing machines is *not* true?

   A few Victorians were aware of the absurdity of them

   B more Victorians enjoyed holidays abroad and preferred Continental bathing huts to English bathing machines

   C gradually they tended to lose their horse and their attendants

   D the biggest change was that they ceased to be moved (by a horse) into the sea

   E by 1914 they were mostly replaced by the modern type of beach-hut

21 The bathing-machines are compared to a 'fringe' in l. 49 because they

   A formed a border to the sea just as a fringe is a border to a dress or a head of hair

   B surrounded the sea as a fringe surrounds a town

   C were just outside the sea just as a fringe of trees might be a small distance away from a road

   D were of doubtful respectability just as 'fringe activities' today are not very moral

   E did not belong to the essential part of the sea just as 'fringe benefits' are not an essential part of one's wages

22 Which ONE of the following words is closest in meaning to 'abrasive' as used in l. 53?

   A tending to graze the skin

   B dangerous to the bather

   C slippery to the feet

   D slimy and unpleasant

   E rough and unsmooth

TRADITIONAL QUESTIONS

Answer the following questions in your own words as far as possible. Questions marked with an asterisk should be answered *very briefly*, and in these answers complete sentences are not necessary.

From Section A

  *1 Give in a single word or short phrase the meaning of *five* of the following words *as used in the passage*.

     i itinerant (l. 4)   **ii** pandemonium (l. 7)   **iii** teeming (l. 9)
     iv hawking (l. 16)   **v** cosmopolitan (l. 18).

  2 Explain the following expressions:
     i 'the din was a constant complaint of contemporaries' (ll. 2–3)
     ii actively or potentially vociferous' (ll. 9–10)   **iii** 'Hearty
     inscriptions' (l. 13).

  3 Why are the words 'artists' (l. 16) and 'professors' (l. 22) in inverted
     commas?

  4 What is the point of the last remark of Section A, 'Highland pipers
     from the glens of Shoreditch' (ll. 24–5)?

  5 Besides noise, what aspects of the Victorian sea-front does the writer
     describe? Use about 40 words.

From Section B

 *6 Give in a single word or short phrase the meaning of the following
     words *as used in the passage:*
     i pumps (l. 7)   **ii** ditties (l. 12)   **iii** verve (l. 16)   **iv** troupes (l. 25).

  7 Show how the following metaphors convey more than plain state-
     ments:
     i 'the hall-mark of the period' (l. 1)   **ii** 'They had a long innings'
     (l. 24)   **iii** 'a stream of touring troupes' (ll. 24–5).

  8 Is the word 'horrible' (l. 32) used literally or metaphorically? Give rea-
     sons for your opinion.

  9 What were the virtues of the 'negro melodists' (l. 2)?

10 What do you understand by the expression 'plantation songs'
     (ll. 10–11)?

From Section C

*11 Give in a single word or short phrase the meaning of *five* of the fol-
     lowing words *as used in the passage*:
     i features (l. 1)   **ii** immutable (l. 5)   **iii** exorbitance (l. 7)
     iv frugality (l. 9)   **v** abuse (l. 36)   **vi** abrasive (l. 53)
     vii peremptorily (l. 56)   **viii** grotesque (l. 62).

12 Show how the following metaphorical expressions convey more than
     plain statements:
     i 'a constant winnowing away of one's tea and sugar' (ll. 18–19)
     ii 'The decoration . . . . was set in a mould' (ll. 24–6)   **iii** 'a solid
     fringe' (l. 49).

13 On what does the remark 'Her numerous grandchildren, apt to have
     whooping-cough or a piano' (ll. 21–2) depend for its humour?

14 Why are the expressions 'respectable woman' (l. 35) and 'brown brandy in her tea' (l. 36) in inverted commas?

15 Write two paragraphs summarizing the information given in the passage about:

   i Seaside landladies and lodging houses *and*
   ii Bathing machines.

The first paragraph should not exceed 120 words in length and the second should not exceed 100 words.

II. Writing English

Write on ONE of the following:

a Give a description of a sea-front that you know, using the methods employed by the writer of the passage in Part I. If you have travelled abroad, use any knowledge you have of foreign seaside towns.
b 'All seaside traders are robbers.' What do you think?
c A boating expedition by sea or river.
d Pirates and piracy.
e Write a story illustrating the saying 'Truth is stranger than fiction'.
f Describe the view from a cliff overlooking a small harbour.

Suggestions for Projects, Assignments and Course Work

1 Dress through the ages—male and/or female—usefulness or decoration—does dress reflect the spirit of the age?—modesty versus display. This piece of work could deal with long periods of time, indicating trends or crazes; or it could deal with a comparatively short period in which dress is related to rank, class, occupation. It could deal with sports attire, showing how different sports have developed suitable dress during the last hundred years.

2 Cowboys and Indians—fact and fiction. Single out individuals such as Billy the Kid, Pocahontas, Wyatt Earp, Buffalo Bill. Refer to films and books. The following may be useful: Mark Twain, *Roughing It*; Hamlin Garland, *The Book of the American Indian*; John Steinbeck, *The Red Pony*; Jack Schaeffer, *Shane*.

3 The Black Death—a documentary or story—read about Eyam in Derbyshire.

III. Using English

Punctuation

Revise uses of semi-colon (between clauses when a longer pause than a comma is needed, or when commas are already in use for a different purpose; between two main statements not joined by a conjunction—never use a comma in these circumstances; to separate and indicate contrast between two main statements joined by such conjunctions as 'but').

1 Punctuate the following passage:

whats the matter i involuntarily asked i beg your pardon sir i was directed to come in is my master not here sir no have you not seen him sir no dont you come from him not immediately so sir did he tell you you would find him here not exactly so sir but i should think he might be here tomorrow as he has not been here today is he coming up from oxford i beg sir he returned respectfully that you will be seated and allow me to do this

2 Section A, Part I contains a list of items separated by semi-colons (ll. 11–24). Section B, paragraph 1 contains a list separated by commas. Account for this difference of punctuation.

3 Account for the following marks of punctuation in the passage in Part I:

i the apostrophe before 'fifties' (l.B. 9) ii the brackets and inverted commas before 'Now' (l.B. 33) and after 'medal' (l.B. 34) iii the hyphens in 'well-to-do' (l.C. 32) iv the colon after 'constant' (l.C. 33) and the colon after 'grotesque' (l.C. 62).

Grammar and Usage

4 Can you justify the use of 'was' (l.C. 7) in view of the subject of the sentence?

5 Would you regard 'Dirt, for one.' (l.C. 10) as a sentence?

6 Write sentences, one for each word, to show you understand the difference in meaning between the words in each pair:

i official, officious ii annoy, aggravate iii affect, effect
iv route, rout.

Spelling and Dictionary Work

7 Use your dictionary to find out the derivation of the following words:

i pandemonium ii baize iii taxi iv goodbye v worry
vi microbe.

8 The following words are incomplete. The dots indicate a letter or letters missing. The number of dots bears no relationship to the number of letters missing. Rewrite the words, spelling them correctly.

i ad . . . ess ii adverti . . . ment iii arg . . . ment
iv defin . . . te v compar . . . tively vi exag . . . rate
vii pos . . . ssion viii med . . . val (of the Middle Ages)
ix mis . . . ell (spell wrongly) x mis . . . se (use wrongly).

Style and Appreciation

9 Show how much of the descriptive effect in Sections A and B of the
passage in Part I is achieved by the use and sometimes repetition of
carefully selected adjectives.

10 The following poem, 'Convoy', by Charles Causley, tells of the death
of a friend on a convoy to Russia in the 2nd World War.

> Draw the blanket of ocean
> Over the frozen face.
> He lies, his eyes quarried by glittering fish,
> Staring through the green freezing sea-glass
> At the Northern Lights.
>
> He is now a child in the land of Christmas:
> Watching, amazed, the white tumbling bears
> And the diving seal.
> The iron wind clangs round the icecaps,
> The five-pointed dogstar
> Burns over the silent sea,
>
> And the three ships
> Come sailing in.

CHARLES CAUSLEY, Union Street (Rupert Hart-Davis)

Divide the poem into sections in order to appreciate it: ll. 1 to 5; ll. 6 to 8;
ll. 9 to 11; and the final couplet. Note Causley's use of unexpected words:
blanket, quarried, iron. What does the final couplet remind you of? Why
is it appropriate?

Books to read

Fame is the Spur	Howard Spring
Huckleberry Finn	Mark Twain
Decline and Fall	Evelyn Waugh
Brighton Rock	Graham Greene
The L-Shaped Room	Lynne Reid Banks
Short Stories	W. W. Jacobs
The Trouble with Lichen	John Wyndham
Seal Morning	Rosemary Farr
The Doctor Syn stories	Russell Thorndike
The Cruel Sea	Nicholas Monsarrat

Unit 9

I. Reading and Understanding

I. Reading and Understanding

Read the following passage (which for your convenience has been divided into three sections) and then answer the questions.

SPACE TRAVEL

[A] Man's first landing on the Moon has been compared in evolutionary importance to the moment when the first fishes crawled out of the sea. Whether this bold comparison is valid will take many thousands of years to prove. But the analogy has one obvious defect in that, unlike the accidental exploration by the   5 fish, man's first step on the Moon was carefully planned over a period of at least a decade, and had been a dream for thousands of years before that. In order to adapt to the new environment of space, we may have to accelerate the tedious march of evolution by performing genetic engineering on our own species.   10

Like the Industrial Revolution, the space age has brought about a radical change in the thinking of our civilization. But unlike the Industrial Revolution, the dawn of the space age can be dated exactly: 4th October 1957. On that day, before many of today's teenagers were born, the Soviet Union orbited the first   15 artificial Earth satellite. Despite clear warnings from the USSR beforehand, the rest of the world was stunned. The first US satellite, due for launch as part of the International Geophysical Year experiments, was still far from ready. (When the first American satellite, Explorer 1, finally did get into orbit on 31st January   20 1958, it weighed a derisory 31 lb in comparison to Sputnik I which weighed as much as a full-grown man.) This comparison had become even worse when in November 1957 Sputnik II carried the dog Laika into orbit in a half-ton capsule.

Two years later the Russians hit the Moon with Luna II and   25 photographed the Moon's far side with Luna III. Then, on 12th April 1961, the Russian Yuri Gagarin became the first man to orbit the Earth. Although the United States had a manned programme under way their intentions in space had been forestalled yet again. The seriousness of the situation, both in propaganda   30 and military terms, seemed obvious to President Kennedy and his advisers. They decided to make the Moon their goal—in the decade of the sixties.

A total of four American astronauts orbited the Earth in one-man Mercury capsules. Although the Soviet Union was orbiting 35 heavier craft, sometimes containing more than one spaceman, by the mid 1960s the United States had catapulted itself into the lead in the so-called space race. This was a result of the two-man Gemini series of flights, which gave US astronauts vital experience in the rendezvous and docking of spacecraft and allowed 40 them to get out of their capsules to work and walk in space. Such feats had to be successfully accomplished before they could be incorporated in the Apollo programme designed to land men on the Moon.

To gather more information about the Moon itself, a series of 45 robot craft, called Surveyor, soft-landed at various points on the lunar surface. They sent back television pictures of their surroundings. Some of the Surveyor probes carried mechanical arms with which to dig the lunar soil, and apparatus with which to analyse the Moon's composition. The general result was that the 50 Moon seemed to be made of a rock similar to basalt, an earthly volcanic rock.

Simultaneously with the Surveyor probes, five Lunar Orbiter craft circled the Moon sending back high-resolution pictures of its entire surface. With this information to hand, spaceflight plan- 55 ners could set about selecting a flat landing spot for the first men. These landing spots were soon needed, since the Apollo system for landing men on the Moon was successfully tried out in the remarkably short space of four flights. Indeed, two missions—Apollo 11 and Apollo 12—put men on the Moon and 60 returned them safely to Earth by the end of 1969, thus doubly fulfilling the late President Kennedy's national commitment.

[B]   The main argument used against spaceflight—that of its cost—is now being attended to. Designs are being worked on for a re-usable vehicle to ferry astronauts into orbit—the so-called space shuttle. At the moment, every multi-million dollar rocket is destroyed as it is used. Astronauts find themselves in the same 5 position as an aviator would who had to build a new aircraft for every flight. Space planners now envisage an aeroplane-like craft that takes off from Earth like a rocket and, having deposited its cargo at the edge of the atmosphere, glides back to land like an aeroplane. After refuelling it would be ready to be used again. 10 With this kind of flight scheme, launch costs could be slashed by well over 90 per cent. Such a space taxi will be particularly valuable because of the coming emphasis on large orbiting workshops from which scientists can study Earth and sky.

What of the stars? Our Sun is, like every other star, dreadfully   15
isolated from its neighbours. Despite this isolation, it is still possible to reach the stars with the rocket power available today—if
we are prepared to wait long enough. By the end of this decade
several unmanned space probes will have left the solar system for
good. Probes planned for launch to the planet Jupiter in 1972 and   20
1973 picked up sufficient velocity by virtue of their close pass to
the giant planet to spin away from the Sun's grip for ever. The
gravitational field of Jupiter is being used in this case like a sling to
accelerate the spacecraft. In the closing years of the seventies the
US space agency NASA plans to launch several space probes on a   25
'grand tour' of the planets, in which all the outer members of the
solar system should be visited. With the extra velocity obtained
being swung round by the planets' gravitational fields, the probes
will leave the solar system and float out towards the stars. The
'escape velocity' from the solar system is only 50 per cent greater   30
than the escape velocity from Earth.

If we were interested in aiming one of these probes towards
Alpha Centauri, the nearest star, the tiny craft would continue on
its journey with no need for extra fuel until it reached its desti-
nation—after about a million years. We could still arrange for a   35
human being to reach the stars after all this time by adopting one
of two systems: either the 'Noah's ark' principle in which gener-
ations are born and die knowing no home other than the spaceship; or the technique called 'hypothermia', in which the
astronauts are kept frozen until a robot brain thaws them out at   40
journey's end. Yet, while we could reach the stars in this fashion, it
is difficult to imagine anyone rash enough to try.

[C]   What we need is a source of power that will continue to accelerate the space ship up to a speed approaching that of light. According to the theory of relativity, the speed of light—186.282
miles per second—is the fastest we can ever hope to go. But, until
we begin to approach this speed, we shall not cut down the transit   5
time to the stars by very much.

A very small acceleration, applied for sufficient time, will
eventually build up a massive final velocity for our spaceship.
The chemical-powered rockets with which we are familiar—the
sort used to launch all the spacecraft to date—certainly do not   10
provide the answer, for the fuel they use is heavy and bulky.
Nuclear or electric powered spacecraft are now under investi-
gation, and may well be the successors of today's cumbersome
rockets. But even these need to carry a power plant on board. If
we can find a source of free energy, then things improve enor-   15
mously.

As it happens, one very obvious source exists—the power of light. Although it may sound incredible, light does exert a certain pressure, and the pressure is partly responsible for the tails of comets streaming away from the Sun. At the edge of the solar 20 system the Sun's light would be too weak to use, but we might consider forming a strong, accurately pointed beam of light by a cluster of lasers—a laser being a kind of super neon tube capable of emitting a beam of light sufficiently powerful when focused by a lens to burn holes in metal. A Canadian engineer has suggested 25 that a giant 'sail' attached to a spaceship could use the pressure of light from an array of lasers parked on Earth to accelerate away to the stars.

Although no one at the moment has any idea how it might be done, there have also been suggestions that the weak forces of 30 gravity or the things between the stars could be harnessed as a source of power. All this, of course, is many years—if not centuries—in the future.

IAN RIDPATH, *Discovering Space* (Shire Publications)

MULTIPLE CHOICE QUESTIONS

After reading each of the following questions, choose the ONE correct answer, and indicate it by writing down the letter that stands for it.

From Section A

1 Which ONE of the following words is closest in meaning to 'valid' as used in line 3?

  A helpful
  B scientific
  C sound
  D effective
  E far-fetched

2 The main idea of the first paragraph is that man's first landing on the moon was

  A a major step forward in man's evolution
  B an attempt to change the direction of man's development
  C thought-out and premeditated for some time beforehand
  D the result of important new techniques in engineering
  E likely to produce, eventually, a new species of man

3 Which ONE of the following words is closest in meaning to 'analogy' as used in line 4?

  A precedent
  B comparison

    C circumstance
    D relationship
    E appropriateness

4 A modern dictionary describes the verb 'to orbit' as an intransitive verb, to revolve, e.g. 'The earth orbits round the sun'. Which ONE of the following remarks is *not* true?

    A in l. 15 'orbited' is used as a transitive verb, meaning 'to cause to revolve'. This is quite different from the dictionary sense

    B in l. 20 'orbit' is used as a noun, so the dictionary entry is irrelevant

    C in l. 28 'orbit' is used as a transitive verb, meaning to 'revolve around'. This is different from the dictionary sense

    D in l. 34 'orbit' is used exactly as in l. 28

    E in l. 35 'orbit' is used exactly as in l. 28

5 Which PAIR of the following sentences best summarizes the two main ideas of paragraph 2 (ll. 11–24)

    i we can give a precise date to the actual beginning of the space age, although outside Russia it was unexpected

    ii in 1957 and for three or four years afterwards the Russians were far ahead of the Americans in space exploration

    iii there are very many similarities between the space age and the Industrial Revolution

    iv the Soviet Union had not warned the rest of the world beforehand that it was going to launch an artificial satellite in 1957

    A i and ii only
    B i and iii only
    C i and iv only
    D ii and iii only
    E iii and iv only

6 Which ONE of the following words is closest in meaning to 'radical' as used in line 12?

    A fundamental
    B important
    C progressive
    D scientific
    E effective

7 Which ONE of the following words is closest in meaning to 'derisory' as used in line 21?

    A comic
    B amusing
    C ironical
    D insignificant
    E futile

8 The decisive advantage in the space race was gained when the

  A Russians launched their first artificial satellite

  B Russians first actually reached the moon with Luna II

  C Russians put the first man into space

  D Americans orbited the earth in one-man capsules

  E Americans learnt to rendezvous space craft and to walk in space

9 The late President Kennedy's national commitment (l. 62) was to

  A put a man into orbit round the earth

  B send a satellite to the moon

  C put a man on the moon before 1970

  D reach another planet

  E prove that space travel was worthwhile

10 The word 'catapulted' (l. 37) suggests

  A jerky starting and stopping

  B a desperate fling

  C a David defeating a Goliath

  D very rapid forward motion

  E an advance stolen secretly

From Section B

11 Which *pair* of sentences best summarizes the two main ideas of paragraph 1 (ll. 1–14)?

  i scientists are devising a rocket that will propel astronauts into space and then return to be re-used

  ii the argument that space travel costs too much ignores the indirect benefits from inventing new materials

  iii re-using the rocket would considerably cut the cost of space exploration

  iv the use of spaceships to carry cargo is seriously being considered

  A i and ii only

  B i and iii only

  C i and iv only

  D ii and iii only

  E iii and iv only

12 The word 'slashed' in l. 1 compares the reduction of costs by over 90 per cent to

  A a cavalryman waving his sword at an enemy

  B an axe removing branches from a tree

  C a sharp instrument cutting all the grass above a certain height

  D a batsman making a wild stroke at a ball

  E a sword wounding a man's flesh

13 Which ONE of the following is closest in meaning to 'envisage' as used in l. 7?

    A assess the advantages of
    B imagine a dream of
    C underestimate the practicability of
    D look forward to the invention of
    E doubt the possibility of

14 'This decade' (l. 18) means

    A this century
    B the next few years
    C this queen's reign
    D this period of ten years, 1970–9
    E this space in time

15 Section B assumes that for a man to reach a star would be

    A almost impossible because it would take so long
    B quite impossible because of the many difficulties
    C highly probable if man resolves to overcome the obstacles
    D very much speeded up by the force of leaving the solar system
    E the ultimate justification of space programmes

16 Which PAIR of the following sentences best describes Section B?

    i it consistently and openly regards the main argument against spaceflight to be its costliness
    ii it moves from discussing the cost of space-travel inside the solar system to the problems of space travel outside it
    iii it moves from the problem of cost to the larger problems of time and space
    iv its main theme is the comparative pointlessness of space travel

    A i and ii only
    B i and iii only
    C i and iv only
    D ii and iii only
    E iii and iv only

17 The purpose of the dash in line 35 is to

    A add the last five words as an afterthought or postscript
    B admit that the formal grammatical structure of the sentence has broken down
    C show that the writer is going to begin his argument again from the beginning
    D end the sentence with a touch of light-hearted humour
    E give the last five words a dramatic emphasis

From Section C

18 As a whole, Section C

 A explains how the difficulties admitted in Section B might possibly be overcome

 B backs up the belief that space travel outside the solar system will always be impossible

 C explains how future space ships may be able to travel even faster than light

 D regards a nuclear—or electric—powered spacecraft as the ideal solution to the problems of space travel

 E gives equal emphasis and probability to several different ways of speeding up a spacecraft

19 Which ONE of the following is closest in meaning to 'cumbersome' as used in line 13?

 A out-of-date and antiquated

 B big and clumsy

 C simple and unsophisticated

 D difficult to manoeuvre

 E costly and uneconomical

20 Which ONE of the following is closest in meaning to 'free' as used in line 15?

 A external to the spaceship

 B costing almost nothing

 C not consuming another type of energy itself

 D external to the solar system

 E that does not add weight to the spaceship

21 Which ONE of the following words is used literally, i.e. not figuratively or metaphorically?

 A 'accelerate' (l. 1)

 B 'cut down' (l. 5)

 C 'streaming' (l. 20)

 D 'parked' (l. 27)

 E 'harnessed' (l. 31)

TRADITIONAL QUESTIONS

Answer the following questions in your own words as far as possible. Questions marked with an asterisk should be answered *very briefly*, and in these answers complete sentences are not necessary.

From Section A

 *1 Give in a single word or short phrase the meaning of *five* of the following words *as used in the passage*:

i bold (l. 3)   ii valid (l. 3)   iii analogy (l. 4)   iv defect (l. 5)
v decade (l. 7)   vi radical (l. 12)   vii derisory (l. 21)
viii forestalled (l. 29).

2   What is the significance of the word 'crawled' (l. 3)?

3   Explain the expressions:
i 'the tedious march of evolution' (l. 9)   ii 'a manned programme'
(l. 28)   iii 'high resolution pictures' (l. 54)   iv 'national
commitment' (l. 62).

4   What do you understand by the expression 'the so-called space race'
(l. 38)?

5   Give the meaning in the passage of the following words which are
now accepted as technical terms of 'space language':
i 'satellite' (l. 16)   ii 'capsule' (l. 24)   iii 'astronaut' (l. 34)
iv 'soft-landed' (l. 46)   v 'probes' (l. 48).

From Section B

6   What is the significance of the word 'taxi' (l. 12)?

7   Why is the expression 'grand tour' (l. 26) in inverted commas?

8   Why is the 'Noah's Ark' principle (l. 37) so called?

9   What reasons does this section put forward for believing that men
will, or will not, ultimately travel to the stars?

From Section C

*10   Give in a single word or short phrase the meaning of the following
words *as used in the passage*:
i 'transit' (l. 5)   ii 'bulky' (l. 11)   iii 'cumbersome' (l. 13)
iv 'plant' (l. 14).

11   What do you understand by the expression 'a source of free energy'
(l. 15)?

12   What does the metaphor 'harnessed' (l. 31) convey that a plain statement would lack?

13   What ways are suggested in this Section by which it might be possible
to speed up the flight of future spaceships?

From the whole passage

14   Pick out five words, usually connected with the sea, which have
become 'space terms'.

II. Writing English

Write on ONE of the following:

a Imagine you are a member of the crew of a space craft. Describe an expedition you take part in.

b Write a science fiction story about the invasion of Earth by 'people' from somewhere in space.

c   'Pawn the whole
Expensive skylark, and put rice in the pot
Bellies of the . . . . . . Scrap it, do you hear?'

These lines are part of a poem by John Moat called 'Overture 58 (in memoriam Grissom, White, Chaffee 27th January 1967)'—the three astronauts were killed by a fire before the rocket left the launching pad. Argue for and against carrying on with an expensive space programme while poverty exists in so many parts of the world.

d Time to spare.

e A description of a cathedral or castle you have visited.

f Africa.

g What impressions of family life are given by radio or television serials? Mention particular programmes, and consider whether they are convincing and true to life.

h Write a story, a description or an essay suggested by the illustration below. (Your composition may be directly about the subject of the illustration, or may only take suggestions from it, but there must be some clear connection between the illustration and the composition.)

Suggestions for Projects, Assignments and Course Work

1 Imagine you are a Member of Parliament. Write a speech in which you defend or attack the expenditure of money on space exploration.

2 You are planning a series of television programmes with the general theme of 'Men against the Elements'. Describe what you are going to do in two or three of the programmes. Show how you link the different parts of the series. Say what people you think of asking to take part. What audience are you aiming at—adults or children, or both?

3 The 1st World War. Deal with one aspect: trench warfare, the war at sea, the beginnings of air warfare, people at home.

The following books might help you: Robert Graves, *Goodbye to All That*; Richard Aldington, *Death of a Hero*; Erich Maria Remarque, *All Quiet on the Western Front*; Siegfried Sassoon, *Memoirs of an Infantry Officer*.

Poems by Rupert Brooke, Wilfred Owen, Siegfried Sassoon.

III Using English

Punctuation

1 Account for the following marks of punctuation in the passage in Part I:

i the comma after 'indeed' (l.A. 59)   **ii** the dashes before 'Apollo' (l.A. 60) and after '12' (l.A. 60)   **iii** the dash after 'today' (l.B. 17) **iv** the commas after 'But' (l.C. 4) and after 'speed' (l.C. 5)   **v** the hyphen between 'chemical' and 'powered' (l.C. 9)   **vi** the inverted commas before and after 'sail' (l.C. 26).

2 Punctuate the following sentences in two different ways as as to produce two different meanings to each sentence. Explain the meaning of each of your sentences.

i When are you going for your walk on Monday   **ii** What do you think I know   **iii** The captain said the major should give the word of command

Grammar and Usage

3 Correct the following sentences where necessary, giving reasons for the corrections you make:

i Due to a late start I will be late for the game.   **ii** Neither of us were able to concentrate on our work.   **iii** I don't approve of you're leaving so early.

4 For each of the following verbs write down a corresponding noun ending in 'sion' or 'tion' (e.g. attend—attention):

i found   **ii** oppose   **iii** declare   **iv** decide   **v** expel   **vi** extend **vii** deceive   **viii** include   **ix** delete   **x** join

5 Construct sentences, one for each word, to show the difference in meaning or usage:

   i obstinate   **ii** resolute   **iii** bigoted   **iv** inflexible.

Spelling and Dictionary Work

6 Use the following words in separate sentences so as to show the difference in meaning between the words in each pair:

   i suit, suite   **ii** stationary, stationery   **iii** sensible, sensitive
   iv respectful, respectable   **v** imaginary, imaginative.

7 Add 'able' or 'ible' to each of the following. Give the meaning of the words you have formed:

   i aud—   **ii** cap—   **iii** not—   **iv** ami—   **v** respons—
   vi vis—   **vii** us—.

Style and Appreciation

8 'It was the best of times, it was the worst of times, it was the age of wisdom, it was the age of foolishness, it was the epoch of belief, it was the epoch of incredulity, it was the season of darkness, it was the spring of hope, it was the winter of despair, we had everything before us, we had nothing before us, we were all going direct to Heaven, we were all going direct the other way—in short, the period was so far like the present period, that some of its noisiest authorities insisted on its being received, for good or evil, in the superlative degree of comparison only.

There were a king with a large jaw and a queen with a plain face, on the throne of England; there were a king with a large jaw and a queen with a fair face, on the throne of France. In both countries it was clearer than crystal to the lords of the State preserves of loaves and fishes, that things in general were settled for ever.'

This is the opening of a novel. What is striking about the style? Is your curiosity aroused by such an opening? Would you be tempted to read on? Do you find the extract humorous? If so, explain what you find to smile at.

Books to Read

The Amateur Astronomer	Patrick Moore
The Promise of Space	Arthur C. Clarke
The Black Cloud	Fred Hoyle
Fallen Star	James Blish
Voyage to Venus	C. S. Lewis
The Day it Rained Forever	Ray Bradbury
Components of the Scene	ed. Ronald Blythe
With a Machine Gun to Cambrai	George Coppard
A Gun for Sale	Graham Greene
The Old Man and the Sea	Ernest Hemingway

Unit 10

I. Reading and Understanding

Read the following passage (which for your convenience has been divided into three sections) and then answer the questions.

THE LAST SURVIVOR FROM FEUDALISM

[A]   Feudalism is a kind of game, set and match with partners at both the serving and receiving ends knowing exactly what is expected of them and abiding unquestionably by the rules. Questioning, in fact, is pointless; it breaks Rule One which is—'accept the lot of the draw'. The last of the old acceptors—on both sides—   5
are, with the exception of Chris Falconer, now in their sixties or seventies and prefer not to see any difference between working for 'Lordship' and working for one of the North Sea Gas projects, or 'him that grows the peas for Birds Eye'. It's all work, they will untruthfully insist. But 'Lordship' and what went with him was   10
far from being all work. A good deal of worship and forgotten mystery managed to interpose themselves in the ritual toil at the manor or 'big house'. Wasn't this where the god lived? And certainly the goddess. 'He was a real gentleman,' said Chris the gardener, 'but Ladyship was *frightening*.' The note of awe and   15
wonder in his voice was familiar enough; one heard it often from aged people in any of the neighbouring Suffolk villages as they tried to describe the particular menace and unpredictability of certain landowners and their wives. It was the duty of a squire to be meaner, odder and richer than any of his equals in the locality.   20
The feudalistic servants seemed to demand this. They also liked to have 'big people' in their particular 'big house'. The Duke of Hamilton who lived in the big house at Easton surrounded by the biggest crinkle-crankle wall in East Anglia was the Zeus of the neighbourhood. The villagers maintain that it was in the cock-pit   25
in his garden that the Jameson raid was planned. His coronet, picked out in gloss paint and cheerfully snowcemmed round, remains fixed to many of the cottages. Lord Covehithe was not quite up to this, being but a baron, but he possessed one mystic card which trumped the county—he was a close friend of King   30
George V. His house lay just outside Akenfield, which had supplied it with servants for centuries. This supply of servants gushed

until 1939, trickled dutifully until about 1950, then abruptly dried
up. After 1950, casual people arrived, at times to suit themselves,
and 'kept the garden down' with park-size mowers and other   35
machines, and on the face of it everything looked as neat as
before. Inside, a Maltese butler wearing suede shoes served dinner
at seven and drove off to Ipswich in his Fiat at eight sharp. On fine
days, Lordship and Ladyship sat on the terrace to a different
silence. 'Once we had worked as if we weren't there,' said Chris.   40
Now, more likely than not, nobody was there. 'I felt sorry for
them,' he added.

[B]   Chris Falconer, the gardener, is an easy, loquacious man
who seems to be ashamed of holding the key feudalistic ideas and
at the same time anxious to put in a good word for them. He uses
the word 'calibre' as a euphemism for the word 'class'—'people of
my calibre . . . people of their calibre'—stocking Suffolk like an   5
arsenal in which the light modern weapon has taken over from the
great crested fieldpiece. He is married with three children and now
works in one of those small, wall-secluded gardens of incredible
perfection which lie behind the streets of Woodbridge. He has the
rather natty good looks of a tail-gunner advertising Brylcreem   10
during the last war which, however, he is young enough to have
missed. His manner is quick and anticipatory. There is in him a
kind of craving to give, to assist, to smooth the path. At less than
fifty, he feels slightly ill at ease in a world which has turned turtle
and encumbered him with a new bungalow, car, television and   15
foreign holidays. He is one of the last generation of initiates of a
social faith whose claims (to use his own staunch ballistic
metaphor) have been exploded. Father, grandfather and great-
grandfather were in service at the big house. Their lives were dedicated to Lordship and Ladyship as totally as other lives have been   20
dedicated to an altar. Chris followed them at fourteen in 1942.
The war was on and the big house with its flagpole and royal mem-
ories focused the local patriotism. Lordship and Ladyship, both
very old, made the most of it. Their refusal to allow 'that dreadful
man' to change a thing in their lives was the talk of the village and   25
one tale of how Ball the butler had been immediately called to restore the vast precision of the dining table after a bomb had disturbed it was much admired. In such a climate it did not seem odd
that Chris should be taken on as trainee under-gardener while
civilization rocked.   30

[C]   Chris apologized for his career in this way:
     I went to Lordship's when I was fourteen and stayed for four-

teen years. There were seven gardeners and goodness knows how
many servants in the house. It was a frightening experience for a
boy. Lord and Ladyship were very, very Victorian and very domi-   5
neering. It was 'swing your arms' every time they saw us. Ladyship
would appear suddenly from nowhere when one of us boys were
walking off to fetch something. 'Swing your arms!' she would
shout. We wore green baize aprons and collars and ties, no matter
how hot it was, and whatever we had to do had to be done on the   10
dot. Nobody was allowed to smoke. A gardener was immediately ·
sacked if he was caught smoking, no matter how long he had
worked there.

   We must never be seen from the house; it was forbidden. And if
people were sitting on the terrace or on the lawn, and you had a   15
great barrow-load of weeds, you might have to push it as much as
a mile to keep out of view. If you were seen you were always told
about it and warned, and as you walked away Ladyship would call
after you, 'Swing your arms!' It was terrible. You felt like somebody with a disease.   20

   The boy under-gardeners had to help arrange the flowers in the
house. These were done every day. We had to creep in early in the
morning before breakfast and replace great banks of flowers in
the main rooms. Lordship and Ladyship must never hear or see
you doing it; fresh flowers had to just be there, that was all there 25
was to it. There was never a dead flower. It was as if flowers, for
them, lived for ever. It was part of the magic in their lives. But the
arrangements were how they wanted them and if one of the gardeners had used his imagination, Ladyship noticed at once and
soon put a stop to it! The guests always complimented her on the   30
flowers and she always accepted the praise as though she had
grown, picked and arranged them herself. It was logical because
servants were just part of the machinery of the big house and
people don't thank machines, they just keep them trim and working. Or that's how I look at it.   35

   In the old days we young men found ourselves quite unable to
talk to Lordship and Ladyship. 'Never speak to them—not one
word and no matter how urgent—until they speak to you,' the
head-gardener told me on my first day. Ladyship drove about the
grounds in a motor-chair and would have run us over rather than   40
have to say, 'get out the way'. We must never look at her and she
never looked at us. It was the same in the house. If a maid was in a
passage and Lordship or Ladyship happened to come along, she
would have to face the wall and stand perfectly still until they had
passed. I wouldn't think that they felt anything about their ser-   45
vants. We were just there because we were necessary, like water

from the tap.

I had a great training as a gardener and acquired all my knowledge completely free. Although I was often horrified by the way
we were all treated, I know I got a terrific amount out of it. It is a   50
gardening background which few people now have, and scarcely
anybody of my age. In a great garden you grow from the seed and
then you see the plant growing where it will always grow, but in a
nursery garden it is just produce and sell, produce and sell. There
is no kind of gardening I can't do. I am not boasting, it is a fact.   55

How can you describe this anxiety we have about our gardens in
Suffolk? I have been to Scotland and they don't have it there. Are
gardens our pride? I think so: it is a breeding in the Suffolk people.
I have never thought about this before but now I would like to get
to the bottom of it. We are all obviously urged to do it as a great   60
necessity in our lives. It is my life. I would die in the attempt to
produce a plant, a flower, and bring it to perfection. But real gardening is dying, dying . . . dying. There aren't many gardeners of
my calibre left. I am a young man who has got caught in the old
ways. I am thirty-nine and I am a Victorian gardener, and this is   65
why the world is strange to me.

RONALD BLYTHE, *Akenfield* (Penguin)

MULTIPLE CHOICE QUESTIONS

After reading each of the following questions, choose the ONE correct
answer, and indicate it by writing down the letter that stands for it.

From Section A

1 By 'feudalism' (l. 1) this writer means a system by which
   A changes in farming techniques and social habits were almost com-
      pletely prevented
   B servants looked up to their landowning masters with great respect
   C employers knew the details of the family life of their servants
   D rich landowners paid too much attention to etiquette and tradition
   E men of the Middle Ages worked and fought for their lord in return
      for protection and the use of land

2 Which ONE of the following comments on the comparisons is *not* true?
   A In ll. 1–2 the feudal relationship between master and servant is
      compared to that between tennis players
   B In ll. 11–14 some of the work that workers did for a 'feudal'
      employer is compared to the action of a religious worshipper
   C In ll. 32–4 the supply of servants is compared to a stream which
      dries up by stages
   D In l. 24 the Duke of Hamilton is compared to the King of the Gods

E   In ll. 38–40 the absence of excitement in the lives of the two old
landowners is compared to an absence of noise

3 The feudal type of employer had all the following qualities with the
ONE exception of

A   being eccentric characters
B   entertaining important guests
C   being much the same as North Sea Gas or a Birds' Eye pea-grower
D   seeming part of a kind of religion
E   filling servants with a kind of terror

4 Chris felt sorry for the lord and lady (ll. 41–2) because, most of all,

A   their children had grown up and left them
B   they did not enjoy other people's company
C   they could no longer live as they were accustomed to
D   their new Maltese butler was so slapdash as to wear suede shoes
E   they had grown old and frail

5 Which two types of silence are compared by the phrase 'a different
silence' (ll. 39–40)?

i   before 1939 the gardeners had to remain unseen and unheard by
their masters
ii   'Lordship and Ladyship' understood one another so well that they
often did not need to speak to one another
iii after 1950 there were no longer any permanent gardeners to make
a noise
iv   noisy machines such as motor mowers were not used

A   i and ii only
B   i and iii only
C   i and iv only
D   ii and iii only
E   iii and iv only

6 To 'accept the lot of the draw' (ll. 4–5) means to

A   recognize the role of chance in life
B   regard one's choice of job as a sort of lottery
C   prefer to work for eccentric aristocratic employers
D   seek to justify class distinctions
E   be content with the class into which one was born

7 Which ONE of the following remarks is *not* true about the working
class in rural Suffolk?

A   till about 1939 they willingly worked for old-fashioned 'feudal'
employers
B   they all stress how workers' relationships with their employers
have changed
C   they used to worship, in some ways, their 'feudal' employers

D they used to expect their employers to be rather angry and threatening

E they were proud to work for employers who knew important people

From Section B

8 'Loquacious' (l. 1) means

A fond of talking

B easy to please

C shy with strangers

D slow of speech

E behind the times

9 Chris Falconer

A although he is about forty retains the attitude to 'feudalism' of older workers

B is dominated by a sense of shame for having been another man's servant

C has an attitude to interviewers very different from his attitude to his employers

D served as a rear gunner in a bomber in the Second World War

E thought it rather slavish to become an under-gardener at fourteen

10 Which ONE of the following words does *not* continue the same metaphor?

A 'calibre' (l. 4)

B 'stocking' (l. 5)

C 'arsenal' (l. 6)

D 'exploded' (l. 18)

E 'focused' (l. 23)

11 During the second World War the local members of the working class

A began to regard 'Lord and Ladyship' as belonging to an out-of-date past

B became more aware how odd and eccentric 'Lord and Ladyship' were

C considered 'Lord and Ladyship' as selfish for still requiring lots of servants

D admired 'Lord and Ladyship' for not allowing Hitler to disturb the details of their life

E talked about 'Lord and Ladyship' less than they used to

12 Lines 18–21 stress that Chris's ancestors

A feared their employers

B respected their employers

C worked hard for their employers

D worshipped their employers

E were loyal to their employers

13 Which ONE of the following does *not* continue the same series of comparisons?

    A 'initiates' (l. 16)
    B 'faith' (l. 17)
    C 'dedicated' (l. 21)
    D 'altar' (l. 21)
    E 'climate' (l. 28)

From Section C

14 Which ONE of the following was *not* true of the conditions under which Chris began work for 'Lordship and Ladyship'?

    A the Second World War had made little difference
    B a very large staff was still kept, both for the garden and the house
    C his employers shouted eccentric orders if they saw him
    D his employers made their staff actually hate them
    E his employers expected their staff to work without ever attracting notice to themselves

15 The tone in which Chris describes these conditions

    A is cool and matter-of-fact
    B never explains how employers came to behave like this
    C expresses his indignation at how he was treated
    D openly stresses how different working conditions were from those of today
    E made him dislike gardens and gardening for the rest of his life

16 Which TWO of the following comparisons make a very similar point?

    i 'You felt like somebody with a disease' (ll. 19–20)
    ii 'It was as if flowers, for them, lived for ever' (ll. 26–7)
    iii 'servants were just part of the machinery of the big house, and people don't thank machines' (ll. 33–4)
    iv 'We were just there because we were necessary, like water from a tap' (ll. 46–7)

    A i and ii only
    B i and iii only
    C i and iv only
    D ii and iii only
    E iii and iv only

17 Chris's strongest feeling about his early career is that it

    A made him unnecessarily shy and cautious
    B demanded the impossible of a young boy
    C taught him a most unusual variety of gardening skills
    D filled him with horror at how his employers behaved
    E made him feel very grateful for a system that protected him from change

18 Which TWO of the following facts justify Chris in calling himself a 'Victorian gardener'? (l. 65)

  i he developed an intense love for perfection in gardens and plants
     that few develop today
  ii he did not have to pay to become apprenticed or to go to technical
      classes in gardening
 iii his cool acceptance of his employers' unfeeling treatment showed
      that he was never afraid of them
 iv he had a Victorian respect for good-manners and etiquette

  A i and ii only
  B i and iii only
  C i and iv only
  D ii and iii only
  E iii and iv only

19 Which TWO of the following are reasons why Chris felt that he needed
    to apologize for his career?
   i he had accepted very calmly a world in which his employers barked
      out unreasonable orders
  ii he now feels that fourteen years is a long time to stay in one job
 iii he did not feel any real indignation at employers who expected
      their servants to behave like machines
 iv he is embarrassed at knowing more about gardening than most
     people whom he talks to

  A i and ii only
  B i and iii only
  C i and iv only
  D ii and iii only
  E iii and iv only

20 Which ONE of the following remarks about the punctuation is *not*
    true?
  A the comma after 'was' in l. 10 introduces what is emphatically a
     new idea
  B the exclamation mark after 'arms' in l. 19 expresses the dictatorial
     tone of the command
  C the commas after 'there' (l. 25) and 'machines' (l. 34) help produce
     a jerky, conversation tone
  D the comma after 'treated' (l. 50) separates off the two (rather con-
     tradictory) halves of the argument
  E the colon after 'so' in l. 58 emphasizes the contrast between the two
     halves of the subject

TRADITIONAL QUESTIONS

Answer the following questions in your own words as far as possible.
Questions marked with an asterisk should be answered *very briefly*, and in
these answers complete sentences are not necessary.

From Section A

*1 Give in a single word or short phrase the meaning of *four* of the following words *as used in the passage*:
   i ritual (l. 12)   **ii** awe (l. 15)   **iii** menace (l. 18)
   iv unpredictability (l. 18)   **v** cheerfully (l. 27).

2 Explain the meaning of the first sentence, showing how the idea of the country squire and his servants is compared with a game of tennis.

3 What was the difference between 'working for "Lordship"' and doing an ordinary job?

4 How can you tell from this section that Chris, the gardener, who is speaking to the author, does not hate the selfish old-fashioned employers whom he is describing? What reasons does he give to explain why most poor workers did not hate their feudal employers?

5 Why was the Duke of Hamilton and Brandon called 'the Zeus of the neighbourhood' (ll. 24–5)?

6 Explain the meaning of the following expressions:
   i 'he possessed one mystic card which trumped the county' (ll. 29–30)
   ii 'kept the garden down' (l. 35).

7 What is the point of the sentence (ll. 37–8) about the butler?

8 Why was the silence 'different' (l. 39)?

9 What does a history book mean by the word 'feudal'? To what extent does this extract use the word in a different sense?

From Section B

*10 Give in a single word or short phrase the meaning of *five* of the following words *as used in the passage*:
   i loquacious (l. 1)   **ii** key (l. 2)   **iii** natty (l. 10)   **iv** anticipatory (l. 12)   **v** dedicated (l. 21)   **vi** climate (l. 28)   **vii** rocked (l. 30).

11 Show how the idea of 'calibre' (l. 5) is developed. Explain the meaning of the sentence 'He uses . . . . crested fieldpiece' (ll. 3–7).

12 Show that the following figurative expressions convey more than plain statements:
   i 'smooth the path' (l. 13)   **ii** 'whose claims had been exploded' (ll. 17–18)   **iii** 'the big house . . . . focused the local patriotism' (ll. 22–3).

13 Why was Christopher Falconer 'slightly ill at ease' (l. 14)? How is this idea continued in the same sentence?

14 Who was 'that dreadful man' (ll. 24–5)? Why, in your opinion, did Lord and Ladyship not name him?

From Section C

  15 Explain the expression 'on the dot' (ll. 10–11).

  16 Is the word 'banks' (l. 23) used literally or metaphorically? Give reasons for your opinion.

  17 Why does Chris call himself a 'Victorian gardener' (l. 65)?

From the Whole Passage

  18 Show how the account of the gardener in his own words (Section C) illustrates some of the statements in Sections A and B.

II. Writing English

Write a composition on ONE of the following:

a Do you think that village life has suffered by the disappearance of most of the country squires of the type described in the passage in Part One? What are the losses, and what are the gains?

b The historical associations of the town in which you live or of a town which you have visited.

c The village shop—can it survive?

d Describe some customs of former times you would like to see revived or retained, and some you are glad no longer continue.

e How wild life is affected by the growth of towns, roads and traffic.

f 'The rolling English road.'

g Just as I turned the corner I saw coming towards me on the wrong side of the road . . . . Continue the story from here.

h Why I should like to become a . . . . Consider the sort of life and work you would like, remembering that some jobs involve indoor or outdoor work, the ability to mix with people, manual skills, quick thinking, perseverance.

Suggestions for Projects, Assignments and Course Work

1 Write a local guide book—an honest one! Each section should deal with a different aspect of your town or village e.g. historic buildings, museums, parks and gardens, entertainment, sport, schools, libraries, and any special facilities. Remember that a guide book is written to encourage and interest visitors; on the other hand, most people appreciate honesty.

2 The 2nd World War. Deal with one aspect e.g. air warfare (the differences between tactics in World War 1 and World War 2, and the reasons)—the war in Africa—the Far East—the atom bomb—the war at home (compare with conditions in the 1914–1918 war).

3 Christmas. Find out how Christmas has become what it is—modern exploitation and commercialism—Christmas cards (origins and development)—Christmas boxes—read John Betjeman's poem 'Christmas'.

III. Using English

Punctuation

1 Account for the following marks of punctuation in the passage in Part I:

   i the dash after 'county' (l.A. 30)   **ii** the hyphen between 'crinkle' and 'crankle' (l.A. 24)   **iii** the commas after 'give' and 'assist' (l.B. 13)   **iv** the brackets before 'to' (l.B. 17) and after 'metaphor' (l.B. 18)   **v** the inverted commas before and after 'that dreadful man' (ll.B. 24–5)   **vi** the exclamation mark after 'it' (l.C. 30).

2 Write sentences to illustrate   **i** one difference between a dash and a hyphen (two sentences)   **ii** the use of a pair of dashes (one sentence)   **iii** the use of a pair of brackets (one sentence).

Grammar and Usage

3 Pronouns stand in place of nouns. Pick out the pronouns in the following sentences and say what kind they are (Personal, Possessive, Reflexive, Demonstrative, Interrogative, Indefinite or Relative):

   i I hope you will visit me before then.   **ii** Whose book is that? It is mine.   **iii** Who was late this morning? I must know who came in after me. Somebody must have done.   **iv** I do not blame you but myself for that accident.

4 Use each of the following words in separate sentences so as to show the differences in meaning:

   i lonely   **ii** alone   **iii** solitary   **iv** desolate   **v** secluded.

5 Use the following words in separate sentences as (a) preposition (b) adverb:

   i by   **ii** near   **iii** over   **iv** under   **v** after   **vi** through   **vii** in   **viii** off.

Spelling and Dictionary Work

6 Write down the plurals of the following words:

   i valley   **ii** potato   **iii** hero   **iv** echo   **v** cargo   **vi** footmark   **vii** oasis   **viii** deer.

7 Find out the derivation of the following words:

   i benevolent   **ii** annihilate   **iii** acrobat   **iv** motel   **v** piano   **vi** sandwich   **vii** cordial   **viii** dandelion   **ix** rifle   **x** rhubarb   **xi** polony   **xii** galore.

Style and Appreciation

8 Sometimes the idea in a metaphor is continued beyond a single word.

This is called sustained metaphor. Pick out one example from Section A (not the first sentence). Show how the metaphor is appropriate.

9 What difference in the style of writing do you see between the first two sections and the last section? Why has the writer changed his style?

10 The following poem is entitled 'Winter Warfare'.

> Colonel Cold strode up the Line
> (Tabs of rime and spurs of ice).
> Stiffened all where he did glare,
> Horses, men, and lice.
>
> Visited a forward post,
> Left them burning, ear to foot;
> Fingers stuck to biting steel,
> Toes to frozen boot.
>
> Stalked on into No Man's Land,
> Turned the wire to fleecy wool,
> Iron stakes to sugar sticks
> Snapping at a pull.
>
> Those who watched with hoary eyes
> Saw two figures gleaming there;
> Hauptman Kälte, Colonel Cold,
> Gaunt, in the grey air.
>
> Stiffly, tinkling spurs they moved
> Glassy eyed, with glinting heel
> Stabbing those who lingered there
> Torn by screaming steel.

EDGELL RICKWORD (Sidgwick & Jackson)

Say in your own words, without the use of personification, what the poet has told us about winter warfare. Pick out two or three lines which you find effective, and say why.

Books to read

Akenfield	Ronald Blythe
Portrait of Elmbury	John Moore
Lark Rise to Candleford	Flora Thompson
Silent Spring	Rachel Carson
Alice's Adventures in Wonderland	Lewis Carroll
Bidden to the Feast	Jack Jones
Jane Eyre	Charlotte Brontë
Death of a Ghost	Margery Allingham
The Wooden Horse	Eric Williams
Time is the Simplest Thing	Clifford D. Simak

Unit 11

I. Reading and Understanding

Read the following passage (which for your convenience has been divided into three sections) and then answer the questions.

BELLRINGING IN ENGLAND

[A] It has been said that to be a ringer in 18th-century England was to be a layabout and a drunk. Whilst this is an exaggerated view, it is true that the standards of behaviour were low. The Commonwealth had discouraged ringing, and from the early 1700s the clergy had virtually vacated the belfry, and ringing was 5 carried out by locals who, in most cases, saw an easy opportunity for earning an extra shilling or two. Ringing being thirsty work, the additional income transferred itself with remarkable speed from the church-tower to the village inn. In town, mainly because of the higher standards of ringing imposed by the various societies 10 and guilds, the situation did not deteriorate to such an extent. Again, because of the denser population near the church, ringing in town was restricted mainly to church feasts and service-ringing, and only the most important secular occasions were commemorated with the bells. 15

But in the rural areas any and every opportunity was taken to ring. Those who rang did so mainly as a hobby and usually for gain—attendance at church services was considered no part of bell-ringing! The arrival of the mail-coach from London was often signalled by the bells, or the squire's birthday celebrated in 20 similar fashion. The village fair was always started off with a spell of ringing, and what with the never-ending series of births, marriages and deaths in the community the ringers were rarely at a loss for an excuse to perform, for which the tavern-keepers were duly grateful. The standard of behaviour in most belfries became 25 appalling. Cursing, swearing and smoking were normal, and in many towers a barrel of beer was always 'on tap' in the ringing-chamber. But this must be viewed in the light of prevailing custom, and was not as scandalous as some writers infer.

Beer was the normal drink of most people in days when the 30 water-supply was anything but safe, and tea and coffee were only for the well-to-do. The Temperance Movement originated in the efforts of brewers to get people to drink beer rather than the pernicious gin that caused such havoc, and, in its early days, the move-

ment did not advocate total abstinence. Beer drinking was taken   35
for granted, as shown by a charmingly candid entry in the parish
accounts of a church in Lancashire: 'Spent on ourselves when we
met at the Abbey Arms to decide how much to give to the Society
for the Propagation of the Gospel'.

Needless to say there are many superstitions connected with   40
bells and ringing. Most of them are associated with death and
burial, and the Passing Bell and the Nine Tailors are well-known.
Despite this they are often confused. The Passing Bell should be
tolled when a parishioner is dying, the Nine Tailors being rung
only when a man finally dies. The name is a corruption from 'tel-   45
lers', and while nine strokes indicated the death of a man, six were
for a woman and three were for the death of a child. From this custom originates the expression 'Nine Tailors make a Man'. During
the nineteenth century there was a fairly general superstition in
rural areas that the soul could not leave the body until the 'tailors'   50
had been rung.

[B]   In many parishes the original use of the bells to signal the
Angelus or Compline became adapted to secular purposes, and in
others new uses for the bells were found. In Louth, Lincolnshire,
bells signalled the beginning of harvesting, and a Harvest Home
Bell announced the safe arrival of the last load. Private individuals   5
often left bequests for ringing to be carried out on special anniversaries. In several parishes, notably Wokingham, Berkshire and
Wingrave, Buckinghamshire, travellers who were lost and who
claimed to have been guided safely home by the bells donated
sums for ringing to commemorate the happy event. But of the   10
many private bequests for ringing to give thanks for timely rescue
from peril, surely the most cynical is that of Thomas Nashe of
Bath. In 1813 this unhappy man left £50 to the Abbey ringers on
condition that they rang a peal with bells muffled 'and the solemn
and doleful changes' on 14th May, this being the anniversary of   15
his wedding, and on the day of his death to ring. ' . . . a grand Bob
Major and merry mirthful peals unmuffled in commemoration of
my happy release from Domestic tyranny and wretchedness'. The
connection between ringing and religion was becoming more and
more tenuous. In the light of this situation, it is not surprising that   20
before long a deep rift developed between ringers and clergy,
amounting, in some parishes, to open hostility. In Devon, for
example, the Rector of Mortehoe was locked out of the church
tower by the ringers, who then changed the lock on the door, and
more than one nervous cleric refused a good living on discovering   25
what sort of ringers controlled the tower.

[C]   Because ringing is a hobby that cannot be practised in isolation but only in co-operation with others, a well-marked social
tradition has developed over the years. Today, in most parishes
this is still seen at its best in the annual ringing-outing, which
usually takes place on a Saturday during summer. The prepara-   5
tion and organization associated with an outing may have taken
most of the winter, and can be a highly frustrating experience for
the person responsible. An outing normally consists of an all-day
tour by coach, visiting perhaps half-a-dozen or more towers
spread over a wide area and ringing 30 or 40 minutes at each.   10
Usually the towers are a considerable distance away, and the day's
trip may well cover a total of 200 miles or more.

In the pages of *The Ringing World* one may find accounts of
ringing-outings and tours during the last fifty years. The journal's
main function, however, is to record peals and quarter-peals suc-   15
cessfully rung, and these are listed under county or diocesan guild
and arranged according to the number of bells in the method. The
name of the ringer of each bell is given, and there is very often a
foot-note giving the reason why the peal was rung. It may be in
honour of a ringer's 21st birthday; to celebrate the engagement or   20
marriage of ringers; to welcome a new incumbent; or to commemorate a church feast. Ringers have not changed a great deal over
the years, and it must be admitted that often the decision is made
to 'go for a peal' and the reason for ringing it decided afterwards!

Unfortunately many younger ringers become obsessed by num-   25
bers, and quantity rather than quality becomes their aim. This
leads to the pernicious practice known as 'tower-grabbing' in
which a small band of ringers tours a district without previous arrangement or warning and tries to ring in as many towers as they
can 'grab' during the day. Occasionally there is news of bands   30
attempting to ring several peals in one day. As a peal takes rather
more than three hours to ring, one must salute the ringers of Hereford for their brawn, if not for their brain, in ringing 5 peals in one
day including one which had to be re-started after 40 minutes'
ringing.   35

JOHN CAMP, *Discovering Bells and Bellringing* (Shire Publications)

MULTIPLE CHOICE QUESTIONS
After reading each of the following questions, choose the ONE correct
answer, and indicate it by writing down the letter that stands for it.

From Section A
   1 The tone with which the writer writes the first paragraph expresses
      A faint amusement
      B considerable indignation

C genuine sadness
D a contempt for religion
E a passionate hatred of drink

2 In which TWO of the following respects did the towns differ from the country?

  i higher standards of ringing were set
  ii fewer people lived near the church
  iii ringing was restricted to fewer occasions ·
  iv the clergy retained more control over bell-ringing

A i and ii only
B i and iii only
C i and iv only
D ii and iii only
E iii and iv only

3 'Secular' (l. 14) means the *opposite* of

A important
B serious
C religious
D traditional
E private

4 The use of an exclamation mark in l. 19 shows that the writer considers the statement he has just made to be

A amusing
B shocking
C surprising
D an afterthought
E a pity

5 Which TWO of the following comments are true of the sentence in ll. 28–9?

  i it questions the accuracy of the facts previously related
  ii it prepares the reader for the main topic of the following paragraph
  iii it sums up the main idea of the paragraph that it ends
  iv it suggests that the stories about bell-ringers' beer-drinking are exaggerated

A i and ii only
B i and iii only
C i and iv only
D ii and iii only
E ii and iv only

6 Which ONE of the following words is closest in meaning to 'deteriorate' as used in line 11?

A alter rapidly
B become worse
C become complicated
D change its nature

  E grow more scandalous

7 All the following contribute to a certain criticism of bell-ringers
EXCEPT

  A 'layabout' (l. 2)
  B 'thirsty work' (l. 7)
  C 'usually for gain' (ll. 17–18)
  D 'appalling' (l. 26)
  E 'prevailing custom' (ll. 28–9)

8 If you were summarizing Section A, which ONE of the following would
you omit?

  A most bell-ringers in 18th-century England drank large quantities
      of beer
  B in town bell-ringing was restricted to fewer occasions
  C beer-drinking seemed a normal activity, safer than drinking intoxi-
      cating gin or unhygienic water
  D most churchgoing people regarded beer-drinking as selfish
  E many superstitions connected bell-ringing with death

From Section B

9 'cynical' (l. 12) means

  A believing the worst of human nature
  B treating serious matters too flippantly
  C unconcerned about other people's feelings
  D indifferent to moral issues
  E unimpressed by the church's teaching

10 'tenuous' (l. 20) means

  A uncertain
  B clear
  C doubtful
  D slight
  E disguised

11 The events dealt with in ll. 20–26 are

  A the contradiction of what has been said previously
  B a cause of what has been said previously
  C the consequence of what has been said previously
  D a further development of what has been said previously
  E a distinct modification of what has been said previously

12 A 'deep rift' (l. 21) is used to describe a feeling that two people are

  A secret enemies
  B aloof but not quite complete enemies
  C very unsympathetic to one another, whether or not they are open
      enemies
  D likely to become open enemies
  E a little ashamed to become open enemies

13 With which TWO of the following does the writer regard the events that he relates in Section B?

   i mild humour
   ii strong indignation
   iii slight disapproval
   iv sad regret

   A i and ii only
   B i and iii only
   C i and iv only
   D ii and iii only
   E iii and iv only

14 Which ONE of the following remarks about the author's use of adjectives is *not* correct?

   A in l. 3 'new' uses include signalling the beginning and end of harvesting and celebrating individuals' happy anniversaries
   B in l. 11 'private' does refer to the uses of bells connected with harvesting because they are not connected with the church
   C in ll. 55–6 'happy' and 'timely' help to include a mild element of humorous exaggeration
   D in l. 17 'mirthful' is repeated by the writer from the original will to help make the matter seem a little comic
   E in l. 25 'nervous' again helps to make the story mildly ridiculous

From Section C

15 The use of the word 'frustrating' in l. 7

   A reads a little oddly because most of Section C stresses how the ringers enjoy their outing
   B prepares us for the next paragraph which stresses how thoroughly such outings are planned
   C emphasizes the contrast between the two halves of the sentence
   D stresses how much bell-ringers have changed since the eighteenth century
   E compares bell-ringing to a kind of obstacle-race

16 In summarizing the main ideas of Section C which ONE of the following would you omit?

   A bell-ringers enjoy going on an annual outing together
   B such an outing normally involves a long round-about journey
   C the details of such outings have changed considerably over the last fifty years
   D the reasons given for ringing some peals are very much like the reasons given by eighteenth-century bell-ringers
   E the ringers of Hereford showed intellectual intiative in ringing five peals in one day

17 Which ONE of the following is closest in meaning to 'become obsessed by' as used in l. 25?

    A grow much too enthusiastic about
    B are attracted to
    C become haunted by
    D have their interest aroused by
    E show distinct preference for

18 'Tower-grabbing' (l. 27) is called 'pernicious' because it

    A shows that the ringers have become too keen on their hobby
    B ruins the nature of the hobby by making it too competitive
    C is an example of selfishness
    D annoys the people who live in the villages
    E gives bell-ringers a bad reputation

19 Section C deals mainly with the

    A factors that make bell-ringing a popular hobby
    B religious significances of bell-ringing
    C reasons (good and bad) why ringers welcome outings
    D ways in which bell-ringing has changed
    E difficulty in obtaining precise information about bell-ringers' unusual feats

20 The writer's attitude towards 'tower-grabbing' (l. 27) is that he

    A disapproves of it strongly
    B pokes fun at it
    C is slightly amused by it
    D is surprised to hear of it
    E cannot understand ringers' motives for joining in it

21 Which ONE of the following words best describes the tone of ll. 22–4?

    A bitter
    B arrogant
    C regretful
    D amused
    E resigned

TRADITIONAL QUESTIONS

Answer the following questions in your own words as far as possible. Questions marked with an asterisk should be answered *very briefly*, and in these answers complete sentences are not necessary.

From Section A

  *1 Give in a single word or short phrase the meaning of *six* of the following words *as used in the passage*:

      i layabout (l. 2) **ii** exaggerated (l. 2) **iii** imposed (l. 10)
      iv deteriorate (l. 11) **v** secular (l. 14) **vi** pernicious (ll. 33–4)
      vii havoc (l. 34) **viii** candid (l. 36).

  2 Explain the expression 'the clergy had virtually vacated the belfry' (l. 5).

3 Why were the standards of ringing higher in towns than in country areas?

4 What were the two main motives for bell-ringing in the eighteenth century?

5 Comment on the expression 'on tap' (l. 27).

6 How did the Temperance Movement begin?

7 What is the meaning of the word 'tellers' (ll. 45–6)?

From Section B

*8 Give in a single word or short phrase the meaning of *four* of the following words *as used in the passage*:
i bequests (l. 6) ii timely (l. 11) iii cynical (l. 12) iv hostility (l. 22) v living (l. 25).

9 Show how the statement 'the original use of the bells . . . became adapted to secular purposes' (ll. 1–2) is illustrated by examples.

10 Explain the meaning of 'The connections between ringing and religion was becoming more and more tenuous' (ll. 18–20).

11 What does the metaphorical expression 'a deep rift developed between ringers and clergy' (l. 21) mean?

From Section C

*12 Give in a single word or short phrase the meaning of *three* of the following words *as used in the passage*:
i frustrating (l. 7) ii function (l. 15) iii commemorate (l. 21) iv obsessed (l. 25) v salute (l. 32).

13 What do you understand by the expression 'a well-marked social tradition' (ll. 2–3)?

14 How does the writer prove that 'Ringers have not changed a great deal over the years' (ll. 22–3)?

15 Explain in your own words what is meant by 'tower-grabbing' (l. 27).

From the Whole Passage

16 By quoting several phrases and then commenting on them show that the writer regards with a mixture of amusement and regret some features of the history of bell-ringing.

17 Summarize in two paragraphs the information given about
i bell-ringers and bell-ringing in the eighteenth and early nineteenth centuries *and* ii ringing outings.

The first paragraph should not exceed 130 words in length and the second should not exceed 50 words.

II. Writing English

Write on ONE of the following:

a Describe either your most amusing experience or your most embarrassing one.
b Tell the story of a bell-ringing outing which failed to achieve any ringing as the result of a succession of accidents.
c 'All hobbies are a profitless waste of time.'
d Winter sports.
e Write short descriptions of the appearance of two quite different people. Relate their appearance to their age, occupation and habits, and place your characters in appropriate settings.
f 'Games are for those who don't read and can't think.'
g Write a story, a description or an essay suggested by the illustration opposite. (Your composition may be directly about the subject of the illustration, or may only take suggestions from it, but there must be some clear connection between the illustration and the composition.)

Suggestions for Projects, Assignments and Course Work

1 Witchcraft—fact and fiction—ancient and modern—black and white magic—read about witches in books—read the witch scenes in *Macbeth*.

2 Imagine your school is to be the subject of a documentary film to last about twenty minutes. Write a script to accompany 'stills' and/or 'movies' which would illustrate what you think are the most important and characteristic aspects of the school. Try to organize your work by a systematic approach dealing with, for example, sport, social activities, teachers and teaching, discipline, pupils' welfare, classrooms and equipment etc.

3 Choose any play you have read, or seen acted. Write a criticism of it which would either encourage or discourage a possible reader or audience. You must say what the play is about, discuss the characters (what kind of people they are—brave, reliable, treacherous etc.) and anything that particularly impressed you.

III. Using English
Punctuation

1 Account for the following marks of punctuation in the passage in Part I:
   i The comma after 'view' (l.A. 3)   ii the comma after 'again' (l.A. 12)   iii the dash after 'gain' (l.A. 18)   iv the exclamation mark after 'bell-ringing' (l.A. 19)   v the comma after 'and' (l.A. 34) and after 'days' (l.A. 34)   vi the colon after 'Lancashire' (l.A. 37)   vii the commas after 'Louth' and 'Lincolnshire' (l.B. 3)   viii the inverted commas before 'and' (l.B. 14) and after 'changes' (l.B. 15)   ix the position of the full stop outside the inverted commas after 'wretchedness' (l.B. 8)   x the apostrophe after 'minutes' (l.C. 34).

2 Insert commas and/or semi-colons as required in the following sentences:

i The savage notices a thunderstorm and trembles at the power it implies but he is ignorant of the electrical currents which are always passing over the earth modifying history profoundly and evincing much more power than a mere flash of lightning.   **ii** It would have been just as well for us two boys if nothing more had been said about the caves but it was fated to be otherwise as I have reason to remember.   **iii** The rope was then thrown John caught it and tied it round me.   **iv** The Chesil Bank for example connecting the peninsula of Portland with the mainland is a mere string of loose pebbles yet it resists by its shelving surface and easy curve the mighty roll of the Channel seas when urged upon the bank by the most furious south-west gales.

Grammar and Usage

3 By any means you choose show the difference between the words or expressions in the following pairs:
i virtually, virtuously   **ii** responsible to, responsible for   **iii** beside, besides   **iv** always, all ways   **v** hear, here.

4 The adverb tells us about the verb, saying how (Manner), when (Time), or where (Place). Adverbs of Degree tell us about adjectives or other adverbs. Pick out the adverbs in the following sentences, say what kind they are and what word they modify (tell us about).
i 'Work hard and play hard' is a good motto.   **ii** I can't work here: it's too noisy.   **iii** I didn't go out yesterday as it was very wet.   **iv** When I ran away I was very quickly followed by my friend.   **v** I am so happy to see you today.

5 Explain the meaning of three of the following expressions:
i a burnt child fears the fire   **ii** to fiddle while Rome burns   **iii** to set the Thames on fire   **iv** to heap coals of fire on.

Spelling and Dictionary Work

6 Use a dictionary to find out the derivations of the following words:
i pernicious   **ii** dairy   **iii** cynical   **iv** daisy   **v** dahlia   **vi** sofa   **vii** sock (short stocking)   **viii** jeans   **ix** Japan   **x** doll   **xi** sherbet   **xi** bangle   **x ii** balcony   **xi** shanty.

7 The following words are incomplete. The dots indicate a letter or letters missing. The number of dots bears no relationship to the number of letters missing. Rewrite the words spelling them correctly.

i insta . . . ent (noun from install)   **ii** g . . . rant . . . (a pledge)
iii priv . . . l . . . ge   **iv** veg . . . tation   **v** c . . . ling (upper limit)
  i har . . . s (worry)   **vii** temp . . . ry   **viii** pref . . . red (liked better)
ix of . . . red   **x** oc . . . red (happened)

Style and Appreciation

8   That was a spring of storms. They prowled the night;
          Low level lightning flickered in the east
          Continuous. The white pear-blossom gleamed
          Motionless in the flashes; birds were still;
          Darkness and silence knotted to suspense,
          Riven by the premonitory glint
          Of skulking storm, a giant that whirled a sword
          Over the low horizon, and with tread
          Earth-shaking ever threatened his approach,
          But to delay his terror kept afar,
          And held earth stayed in waiting like a beast
          Bowed to receive a blow. But when he strode
          Down from his throne of hills upon the plain,
          And broke his anger to a thousand shards
          Over the prostrate fields, then leapt the earth
          Proud to accept his challenge; drank his rain;
          Under his sudden wind tossed wild her trees;
          Opened her secret bosom to his shafts;
          The great drops spattered; then above the house
          Crashed thunder, and the little wainscot shook
          And the green garden in the lightning lay.

The above is an extract from 'The Land' by V. Sackville-West. Write an appreciation, paying particular attention to the imagery (this includes the figures of speech), the use of contrast, and the effect of alliteration and onomatopoeia. Note the punctuation. Show that the sequence of events is true to life.

Books to read

Short Stories	Frank O'Connor
Whisky Galore	Compton Mackenzie
Billy Liar	Keith Waterhouse
Rebecca	Daphne du Maurier
The Jungle	Upton Sinclair
Up into the Singing Mountain	Richard Llewellyn
The Trumpet Major	Thomas Hardy
Land Below the Wind	Agnes Newton Keith
Three Men in a Boat	Jerome K. Jerome

Unit 12

I. Reading and Understanding

Read the following passage (which for your convenience has been divided into two sections) and then answer the questions.

MONDAY MORNING IN THE CYCLE FACTORY

[A] The bright Monday-morning ring of the clocking-in machine made a jarring note, different from the tune that played inside Arthur. It was dead on half-past seven. Once in the shop he allowed himself to be swallowed by its diverse noises, walked along lanes of capstan lathes and millers, drills and polishers and   5 hand-presses, worked by a multiplicity of belts and pulleys turning and twisting and slapping on heavy well-oiled wheels overhead, dependent for power on a motor stooping at the far end of the hall like the black shining bulk of a stranded whale. Machines with their own small motors started with a jerk and a whine under   10 the shadows of their operators, increasing a noise that made the brain reel and ache because the weekend had been too tranquil by contrast, a weekend that had terminated for Arthur in fishing for trout in the cool shade of a willow-sleeved canal near the Balloon Houses, miles away from the city. Motor-trolleys moved up and   15 down the main gangways carrying boxes of work—pedals, hubs, nuts and bolts—from one part of the shop to another. Robboe the foreman bent over a stack of new time-sheets behind his glass partition; women and girls wearing turbans and hairnets, and men and boys in clean blue overalls, settled down to their work, eager   20 to get a good start on their day's stint; while sweepers and cleaners at everybody's beck and call already patrolled the gangways and looked busy.

    Arthur reached his capstan lathe and took off his jacket, hanging it on a nearby nail so that he could keep an eye on his belong-   25 ings. He pressed the starter button, and his motor came to life with a gentle thump. Looking around, he could not see, despite the infernal noise of hurrying machinery, that anyone appeared to be working with particular speed. He smiled to himself and picked up a glittering steel cylinder from the top box of a pile beside him,   30 and fixed it into the spindle. He jettisoned his cigarette into the sud-pan, drew back the capstan, and swung the turret on to its

broadest drill. Two minutes passed while he contemplated the
precise position of tools and cylinder; finally he spat on to both
hands and rubbed them together, then switched on the sud-tap   35
from the movable brass pipe, pressed a button that set the spindle
running, and ran in the drill to a neat chamfer. Monday morning
had lost its terror.

At a piecework rate of four-and-six a hundred you could make
your money if you knocked-up fourteen hundred a day—possible   40
without grabbing too much—and if you went all out for a thousand in the morning you could dawdle through the afternoon and
lark about with the women and talk to your mates now and again.
Such leisure often brought him near to trouble, for some weeks
ago he stunned a mouse—that the overfed factory cats had   45
missed—and laid it beneath a woman's drill, and Robboe the
gaffer ran out of his office when he heard her screaming blue-
murder, thinking that some bloody silly woman had gone and got
her hair caught in a belt (big notices said that women must wear
hairnets, but who could tell women?) and Robboe was glad that it   50
was nothing more than a dead mouse she was kicking up such a
fuss about. But he paced up and down the gangways asking who
was responsible for the stunned mouse, and when he came to
Arthur, who denied having anything to do with it, he said: 'I'll bet
you did it.' 'Me, Mr Robboe?' Arthur said, the picture of inno-   55
cence, standing up, tall with offended pride. 'I've got so much
work to do I can't move from my lathe. Anyway, I don't believe in
tormenting women, you know that. It's against my principles.'
Robboe glared at him: 'Well, I don't know. Somebody did it, and
I reckon it's you. You're a bit of a Red if you ask me, that's what   60
you are.' 'Now then, that's slander,' Arthur said. 'I'll see my law-
yers about you. There's tons of witnesses.' Robboe went back to
his office, bearing a black look for the girl inside, and for any tool-
setter that might require his advice in the next half hour; and
Arthur worked on his lathe like a model of industry.   65

[B]   Though you couldn't grumble at four-and-six a hundred the
rate-checker sometimes came and watched you work, so that if he
saw you knock up a hundred in less than an hour Robboe would
come and tell you one fine morning that your rate had been
dropped by sixpence or a bob. So when you felt the shadow of the   5
rate-checker breathing down your neck you knew what to do if
you had any brains at all: make every move more complicated,
though not slow because that was cutting your own throat, and do
everything deliberately yet with a crafty show of speed. Though
cursed as public enemy number one, the rate-checker was an inno-   10

cuous-looking man who carried a slight stoop everywhere he went and wore spectacles, smoking the same fags as you were smoking, and protecting his blue pinstriped suit with a brown stall overall, bald as a mushroom and as sly as a fox. They said he got com- 15
mission on what reductions he recommended, but that was only a rumour, Arthur decided, something said out of rancour if you had just been done down for a bob. If you saw the rate-checker on your way home from work he might say good evening to you, and you responded to this according to whether or not your rate had been tampered with lately. Arthur always returned such signs with 20
affability, for whenever the rate-checker stood behind him he switched his speed down to a normal hundred, though once he had averaged four hundred when late on his daily stint. He worked out for fun how high his wages would be if, like a madman, he pursued this cramp-inducing, back-breaking, 25
knuckle-knocking undiplomatic speed of four hundred for a week, and his calculations on the *Daily Mirror* margins gave an answer of thirty-six pounds. Which would never do, he swore to himself, because they'd be down on me like a ton of bricks, and the next week I'd be grabbing at the same flat-out lick for next to 30
nowt. So he settled for a comfortable wage of fourteen pounds. Anything bigger than that would be like shovelling hard-earned money into the big windows of the income-tax office—feeding pigs on cherries, as Mam used to say—which is something else against my principles. 35

So you earned your living in spite of the firm, the rate-checker, the foreman, and the tool-setters, who always seemed to be at each other's throats except when they ganged-up to get at yours, though most of the time you worked quite happily for a cool four- teen nicker, spinning the turret to chamfer in a smell of suds and 40
steel, actions without thought so that all through the day you filled your mind with vivid and more agreeable pictures than those round about. It was an easier job than driving a lorry, for instance, where you had to have your wits about you. Now whole days could be given up to woolgathering. Hour after hour quickly 45
disappeared when once you started thinking, and before you knew where you were a flashing light from the foreman's office signalled ten o'clock, time for white-overalled women to wheel in tea urns and pour out their wicked mash as fast as they could from a row of shining taps. 50

ALAN SILLITOE, *Saturday Night and Sunday Morning* (W. H. Allen)

MULTIPLE CHOICE QUESTIONS

After reading each of the following questions, choose the ONE correct answer, and indicate it by writing down the letter that stands for it.

From Section A

1 After a weekend spent mostly in fishing, Monday morning in the factory was a
 A stimulating change
 B return to real purpose
 C noisy shock
 D welcome opportunity to make money
 E depressing anticlimax

2 Which ONE of the following phrases does *not* stress the noise in the factory?
 A 'a jarring note' (l. 2)
 B 'swallowed by its diverse noises' (l. 4)
 C 'slapping on heavy well-oiled wheels' (l. 7)
 D 'started with a jerk and a whine' (l. 10)
 E 'motor trolleys moved up and down the main gangways' (ll. 15–16)

3 The author obviously regards fishing (l. 13) as a pursuit that is
 A trivial
 B selfish
 C boring
 D soothing
 E urban

4 'Monday morning had lost its terror' (ll. 37–8) because Arthur
 A had made sure that his machine was working
 B saw that other workers were working faster than he was
 C had finished his first hesitant preliminary actions
 D had become genuinely eager to work
 E had decided to win the foreman's approval

5 Robboe, the foreman, is portrayed as
 A coolly efficient
 B something of a bully
 C too devoted to the factory's welfare
 D very hardworking
 E easily harassed

6 When Arthur worked on his lathe 'like a model of industry' (l. 65) he
 A had become more enthusiastic about work
 B had decided to carry out the plan he had formulated in ll. 41–3
 C was merely trying to deceive the foreman
 D was showing how interesting his work normally was
 E was positively afraid of getting the sack

7 Which ONE of the following phrases does *not* stress the unpleasant aspect of factory life?

A 'a jarring note' (l. 2)
B 'swallowed by its diverse noises' (l. 4)
C 'dependent for power on a motor' (l. 8)
D 'like the black shining bulk of a stranded whale' (l. 9)
E 'with a jerk and a whine' (l. 10)

8 Arthur's attitude towards the factory is fundamentally

A contented
B bored
C neutral
D defiant
E despondent

9 Robboe went back to the office with a black look because he

A had failed to get Arthur to own up
B was absolutely sure that Arthur was a kind of rebel
C was himself genuinely afraid of mice
D was shocked that women workers should be frightened by Arthur's prank
E believed that the workers were wasting too much time

10 In l. 55 ONE of the following best fits the tone of voice in which Arthur used to ask, 'Me, Mr. Robboe?'

A he complained
B he urged
C he protested
D he pleaded
E he insisted

From Section B

11 'That your rate had been dropped by sixpence or a bob' (l. 5) means that you

A earned a smaller wage at the end of the week
B earned less for doing the same amount of work in a given time
C earned less because you were now working more slowly
D were not expected to do so much work in the allotted time
E had been transferred to a job demanding less skill

12 The use of the word 'shadow' in l. 5 suggests that the rate-checker

A was threatening Arthur with dismissal
B had become Arthur's inseparable companion
C was so similar to Arthur as to seem his reflected image
D threatened the arrival of future difficulties for Arthur
E seemed an unsubstantial and unreal thing to Arthur as he day-dreamed

13 'Yet with a crafty show of speed' (l. 9) means

A working faster when the rate-checker is watching
B temporarily attaining your maximum speed
C pretending to work nearer to your maximum speed than you really are
D speeding up when you are being watched
E making the job look easier than it really is

14 Which ONE of the following is closest in meaning to 'innocuous' in l. 10?
A harmless
B offensive
C insignificant
D good-tempered
E efficient

15 Which ONE of the following words is closest in meaning to 'rancour' as used in l. 16
A indignation
B resentment
C spitefulness
D suspicion
E surprise

16 Which ONE of the following phrases is to be taken literally (as opposed to figuratively)?
A 'your rate had been dropped' (ll. 4–5)
B 'that was cutting your throat' (l. 8)
C 'carried a slight stoop' (l. 11)
D 'protecting his pin-striped suit' (l. 13)
E 'your rate had been tampered with' (ll. 19–20)

17 Which ONE of the following is closest in meaning to 'affability' as used in l. 21?
A hypocrisy
B pretence
C courtesy
D irony
E heartiness

18 Which ONE of the following words best describes the tone in which Arthur talks to himself about the rate-checker?
A bitter
B arrogant
C disdainful
D angry
E understanding

19 The 'speed' (l. 26) would be 'undiplomatic' because it would

A   reveal how fast the job could be done
B   endanger his health
C   make life difficult for other workers
D   lead Arthur into rash behaviour
E   mark the end of Arthur's caution

20   The use of the word 'settled' in l. 31 suggests that Arthur is

A   driving a bargain
B   establishing a permanent way of life
C   making up his mind
D   fixing his mind on his work
E   accepting a compromise

21   The flashing light from the foreman's office (l. 47) is a symbol of how

A   mechanical are the arrangements in the factory
B   glad the workers are to have a tea-break
C   resolved the employers are to study their workers' welfare
D   quickly time passes when working in a factory
E   refined is the split-timing of factory management

22   The essential point of Arthur's attitude to work is that he is

A   just a little afraid of Robboe the foreman
B   indignant that he is being exploited by his employers
C   bored with the repetitive nature of his work
D   hard pushed to maintain the speed of work enforced by the rate-checker
E   resolved to limit the physical and mental effort that he puts into it

23   All these statements are true about Section B EXCEPT that it

A   gives us the thoughts passing through the mind of a character in a novel
B   is more interested in workers' psychological reactions than in whether they are adequately paid
C   stresses how unfairly the factory owners treat their workers
D   reminds us that the monotonous simplicity of factory work appeals to some workers for some of the time
E   includes a certain amount of witty humour

24   The reader sympathizes with Arthur for all the following EXCEPT for the fact that he

A   is pitting his wits against those of the rate-checker
B   does not feel any personal bitterness towards the rate-checker
C   shares a common reluctance to earn extra money that will be heavily taxed
D   is unfairly suspected by his superiors
E   obviously enjoys many aspects of life

25   To Arthur day-dreaming is a

    A futile way of wasting time
    B pleasure which factory-work makes easy
    C desperate retreat from the unpleasantness of reality
    D special treat which he keeps for certain times
    E way of expressing his defiance of the rate-checker and the foreman

TRADITIONAL QUESTIONS

Answer the following questions in your own words as far as possible. Questions marked with an asterisk should be answered *very briefly*, and in these answers complete sentences are not necessary.

From Section A

*1 Give in a single word or short phrase the meaning of *five* of the following words *as used in the passage*:

    i jarring (l. 2) **ii** diverse (l. 4) **iii** patrolled (l. 22) **iv** infernal (l. 28) **v** jettisoned (l. 31) **vi** dawdle (l. 42).

2 What aspects of the factory affect Arthur most as he enters it?

3 Why did Arthur enjoy fishing at the weekend?

4 Why does Arthur not work as hard as he could?

5 Describe the attitudes of Arthur and the foreman to each other.

6 What is the significance of the expressions:

    i 'Monday morning had lost its terror' (ll. 37–8) **ii** 'You're a bit of a Red' (l. 60)?

7 Pick out one simile and show how it helps the writer to convey his point of view.

8 What do you understand by the use of the following expressions in their context:

    i 'swallowed' (l. 4) **ii** 'lanes' (l. 5) **iii** 'willow-sleeved' (l. 14)?

*9 Pick out TWO examples of deliberate exaggeration for effect (hyperbole).

From Section B

*10 Give in a single word or short phrase the meaning of *four* of the following words *as used in the passage*:

    i innocuous (l. 10) **ii** rancour (l. 16) **iii** affability (l. 21) **iv** stint (l. 23) **v** woolgathering (l. 45).

11 Identify a sentence that expresses Arthur's unspoken thoughts. Briefly justify your choice.

12 Pick out TWO similes and show how effective they are.

13 What do you understand by the expression 'feeding pigs on cherries' (ll. 33–4)? Why is it used here?

14 What was Arthur's attitude towards the rate-checker? Use not more than 40 words.

15 Explain the significance of the adjectives in the following expressions:

   i 'fine morning' (l. 4)   ii 'undiplomatic speed' (l. 26)   iii 'wicked mash' (l. 49).

16 Why does Arthur not change his job? What is his attitude towards to life?

17 Explain the following expressions as used in the passage:

   i 'cutting your own throat' (l. 8)   ii 'always seemed to be at each other's throats' (ll. 37–8).

II. Writing English

Write on ONE of the following:

a Write a description of a different sort of factory from that in which Arthur works. Include internal and external features in your account, the relations of workers to employers, and any social activities, if such exist.

b What are your views about going on holiday with your family?

c Television has discouraged all indoor and many outdoor hobbies and activities. What are your views?

d What do you want from your career? And what are you prepared to give?

e Tea with my aunts.

f Write a letter to a friend describing a journey by caravan (either the modern caravan or the gipsy type).

g Describe a small fishing village *or* a large seaside resort *or* a busy port. Make use of the seasons, the weather, and times of day and night in your account, and introduce suitable characters to give credibility to your description.

h Write a story suggested by the following lines by Patricia Beer:

'I told them not to ring the bells
The night the Vikings came
Out of the sea and passed us by.'

Suggestions for Projects, Assignments and Course Work

1 Advertising. Show how we are 'pressured' into buying certain articles—show how advertisers use fear, vanity, ambition, jealousy and

flattery to persuade us. What are the advantages of advertising to **a** the advertisers **b** the public? Is honesty the best policy in advertising?

Invent names for a new hair cream for men, a new washing powder, a new weekly magazine (mention the readers for whom it is intended), and a new proprietary medicine.

Write an advertisement for three of these, appealing in each case to fear or ambition or vanity.

2 Tell how you helped in an archaeological dig. Give an account of the procedure and describe some of your finds.

III. Using English

Punctuation

1 Each of the following sentences contains one error in punctuation. Identify it and explain why it is an error.

  i The centre-forward, who scored most goals in the First Division this season is only eighteen.
  ii The sudden descent of the fog, took most drivers by surprise.
  iii To sell a faked chair as a genuine antique is dishonest, today it also contravenes the Trades Descriptions Act.
  iv The old squire—he used to play cricket for Suffolk years ago, is still chairman of the village cricket club.
  v He asked me whether I would like to drive his car?
  vi I asked the village greengrocer, 'Can you show me the way to Naseby'?
  vii Manchester United were the 'glamour' side of the 1950s'.
  viii I traced the River Welland almost to it's source.

2 Account for the following marks of punctuation in the passage in Part I:
  i the dashes before 'pedals' (l.A. 16) and after 'bolts' (l.A. 17)   **ii** the semi-colons after 'partition' (l.A. 18) and after 'stint' (l.A. 21)   **iii** the commas after 'together' (l.A. 35), 'pipe' (l.A. 36) and 'running' (l.A. 37)   **iv** the dashes before 'that' (l.A. 45) and after 'missed' (l.A. 46)   **v** the comma after 'anyway' (l.A. 57)   **vi** the colon after 'all' (l.B. 7)   **vii** the commas after 'cramp-inducing' (l.B. 25) and 'back-breaking' (l.B. 25)   **viii** the dashes before 'feeding' (l.B. 33) and after 'say' (l.B. 34).

Grammar and Usage

3 Use each of the following words in separate sentences in such a way as to bring out the difference in meaning between them:
  i ask   **ii** request   **iii** beg   **iv** demand   **v** petition

4 Give the meaning of the prefix in each of the following words:
  i antedate   **ii** antidote   **iii** precede   **iv** connect   **v** surcharge
  vi autograph   **vii** biscuit   **viii** object   **ix** perimeter   **x** telescope

5 Use the following in separate sentences (two sentences for each pair) so as to bring out the difference in meaning between the first word and the second word or phrase in each pair:

i already, all ready   **ii** recount, re-count   **iii** altogether, all together   **iv** everyone, every one.

Spelling and Dictionary Work

6 Use your dictionary to find the derivation of the following words:

i jungle   **ii** castanets   **iii** leper   **iv** dynamite   **v** crony
vi lunatic   **vii** bugle   **viii** pawn (in chess)   **ix** hippodrome
x foolscap.

7 The dots in the following words represent missing letters, but the number of dots does not represent the number of letters required. Write out each word correctly spelt.

i di . . . appear   **ii** bel . . . ve   **iii** di . . . atisfied   **iv** uncon . . . ious
v independ . . . nt   **vi** Brit . . . n (the country)   **vii** par . . . l . . . l
viii medi . . . val   **ix** priv . . . lege   **x** quarr . . . ling   **xi** twel . . . h
xii ski . . . ful   **xiii** rec . . . pt   **xiv** ach . . . ve.

Style and Appreciation

8 The writer of the passage in Part I deliberately varies his style. Quote from the passage to show three different styles of writing and account for the differences. Note the difference in length of sentences, the use of repetition, the words used (vocabulary), colloquialisms (words used mainly in speech), figures of speech. Pick out FIVE colloquial or slang expressions and explain what they mean.

9 Look up the following words in your dictionary and try to invent or remember examples:

i palindrome   **ii** malapropism   **iii** parody   **iv** pun   **v** spoonerism.

Books to read

The History of Mr. Polly	H. G. Wells
Kipps	H. G. Wells
Anna of the Five Towns	Arnold Bennett
The Mayor of Casterbridge	Thomas Hardy
How Green was My Valley	Richard Llewellyn
Desperate Voyage	John Caldwell
The Kraken Wakes	John Wyndham
Man Meets Dog	Konrad Lorenz
Short Stories	Paul Gallico
The Day of the Triffids	John Wyndham

Unit 13

I. Reading and Understanding

Read the following passage (which for your convenience has been divided into three sections) and answer the questions.

DUCKS

[A]   Ducks are most active in the early morning and evening when they fly to and from their feeding or resting grounds, often spending a good deal of the day in sleep if not disturbed. The sur-face-feeding ducks are able to feed in the dark if compelled to do so, but the diving ducks usually obtain their food in daylight and   5
therefore suffer if they have not sufficient peace to feed during the day.

   In most species of northern ducks the plumage of the males is much brighter and more varied in colour than that of the females, who need to be dull and inconspicuous when incubating the eggs.   10
The plumage of the Sheld-duck is similar in duck and drake, but as these birds usually nest in holes it is not necessary for the duck to be inconspicuous. Unlike ganders, which are most devoted parents, drakes take little interest in their families and in most of the northern species retire to moult when the incubation of the   15
eggs begins, though some of them assist in the care of the young. This moult brings the drake into 'eclipse' plumage which closely resembles that of the female. He, however, remains in this state only for a short time and by winter has regained his handsome ap-pearance.   20

   A distinctive feature among almost all ducks is a little patch of coloured feathers in the wing which is called the 'speculum'. This varies in each species, and also in some cases between the sexes of the same species, and is a helpful means of identification.

   Ducks are sociable birds, generally congregating in flocks, and   25
several species, such as Mallard, Teal, Wigeon, Pintail and Shoveller, may be seen on the water together. Pochard and Tufted also assemble together in flocks. Sheld-duck are more inclined to keep in parties of their own, and in some places will congregate in enormous flocks; I have seen as many as ten thousand of these   30
birds together in winter on the island of Terschelling, off the north coast of Holland.

Ducks do not, however, usually nest in colonies, though the Eiders do so, often in large numbers, and it is contended by some ornithologists that diving duck are more inclined to nest together.   35

[B]   The psychology of ducks is a study with great possibilities. That they have a distinct sense of play is obvious from the way they disport themselves in the water and catch at flies. This sense of play is further developed in the displays given by drakes during the breeding season, such as nodding their heads, stretching   5 their necks, spreading their wings, and other methods designed to attract the female ducks. These displays culminate in the elaborate performance given by the Goldeneye, which uses its beak, head and tail all at once, at the same time rapidly striking the water backwards with its feet in a complicated movement.   10 Sheld-ducks have realized the uses of a community and are inclined to pool their families and thus rid themselves of undue cares. I have watched several families of young Sheld-duck under the care of two adults in the corner of a mere in Norfolk while the rest of the birds led a carefree existence. They also   15 seem to have some reasoning power, which was shown at the same place, though I did not witness it myself. A pair of Sheld-ducks had nested some distance away and the father, having far to walk to take the ducklings to the water, carried one of the youngsters on his back. The entrance to the mere is barred by a   20 gate and this presented a difficult problem; but after a moment's hesitation the parent deposited the youngster on the ground, squeezed under the gate and waited on the other side for the duckling to get on his back again. Wigeon are opportunists, and I have seen them in sedulous attention on a Swan, waiting for it to bring   25 up succulent stems from far under water, which they seize before the Swan can eat them itself. Spite is also evident in some birds. I have watched a lone drake Mallard continually harry and chase a female of the same species and her family, attempting to head off and drown one of the youngsters by seizing it with his beak.   30

The young of duck are most attractive and are all able to swim and dive soon after leaving the shell. They are clad in long fluffy down, and the usual colour scheme of most species is a lightish colour with dark stripes or markings. Mortality among young ducks is very great, for they have many enemies, particularly rats,   35 pike, otters, gulls and crows. No doubt for this reason ducks usually lay large clutches of eggs.

The beaks of ducks are most distinctive and vary a certain amount among the species, the diving ducks having them on the whole somewhat longer than the surface-feeders. Some, such as   40

the Goldeneye, Pochard, Tufted and Scaup, possess a broad bill with a narrow 'nail', as the small bony protuberance on the tip is called; others such as the Eider duck possess a broad bill with a broad nail. The Saw-bills have, of course, narrow slender bills with sharp teeth. The heavy spatulate bill of the Shoveler is very   45
characteristic of the bird and not like that of any other duck.

[C]   Ducks are found all over Great Britain where there is fresh or salt water and suitable feeding grounds. The choice can be made whether to pursue them to their wild retreats to observe them, or to take the more easy line and watch them on the big reservoirs where they will congregate in hordes. Even the rarest   5
species will come quite close to towns—I have seen Smew on a reservoir as near London as the neighbourhood of Hammersmith Bridge, and each year records of interesting species are made in London. The main difficulty about watching duck in the truly wild state is that they are usually so far away and the   10
light is so often wrong: they always seem to be on the other side of the estuary or lake, and invariably between you and the sun if there is any sun. The most satisfactory means of observation is by telescope, but this is not easy in a wind; with powerful field-glasses, however, a lot can be achieved. The flight of duck is also   15
characteristic, and it is sometimes easier to identify them on the wing than when bunched in big flocks on the water. But the very difficulties that have to be countered make the study of duck all the more enthralling, and wet feet, cold and fatigue are forgotten in the excitement of seeing vast congregations of these birds,   20
identifying the different species and watching them carrying out their various pursuits. I have often heard people say that they cannot understand how some can love wildfowl and shoot them, but in my experience I have usually found that those who shoot wildfowl know far more about them than most other people, and   25
from the duck's point of view, though it is not at first apparent, are among his best friends, for they are the keenest to preserve him and know how to do so in the most practical way.

PHYLLIS BARCLAY-SMITH, *A Book of Ducks* (Penguin)

MULTIPLE CHOICE QUESTIONS
After reading each of the following questions, choose the ONE correct answer, and indicate it by writing down the letter that stands for it.

From Section A

1 Which ONE of the following remarks applies to all ducks rather than to a specific type of them?

A they can feed in the dark if·they are forced to
B the males have more brightly-coloured feathers than the females
C they like to spend much of the middle part of the day in sleep
D they tend to form large flocks of their own kind
E they nest in very large groups

2 Which ONE of the following distinctions is *not* made in this section?

A between those ducks which feed on the surface and those which dive for food
B between male ducks and female ducks
C between those ducks which nest in holes and those which do not
D between those ducks which congregate with other types of duck and those which do not
E between those ducks which look after their families and those which do not

3 Which ONE of the following remarks about male ducks (drakes) is not true?

A they usually have brighter coloured feathers
B they usually are more conspicuous than the females
C they take very little interest in their young
D they look very unlike the females during nesting time
E they are easily distinguished from the females during the winter

4 Which ONE of the following remarks does the writer make most confidently and dogmatically?

A 'Ducks are most active in the early morning and evening' (l. 1)
B 'the diving ducks usually obtain their food in daylight' (l. 5)
C 'This varies . . . . in some cases between the sexes of the same species' (ll. 22–4)
D 'Sheld-duck are more inclined to keep in parties of their own' (ll. 28–9)
E 'it is contended by some ornithologists that diving duck are more inclined to nest together' (ll. 34–5)

5 'Contended' (l. 34) means

A believed
B denied
C imagined
D argued
E contested

6 The drake's loss of bright feathers is compared to an eclipse of the sun (l. 17) because it

A recurs regularly
B involves a temporary loss of brilliance
C reduces the male to the same level as the female
D makes the drake more difficult to see
E reminds one that ultimately the sun will burn out

7 'A distinctive feature' (l. 21)

   A stresses the characteristics that ducks share with other birds
   B is an example of an unexplained feature in ducks
   C emphasizes the differences between ducks and other birds
   D cannot be attributed to any logical reason
   E helps to perpetuate the species

8 If you were briefly summing up the subject-matter of this passage, which ONE of the following would you omit?

   A ducks' feeding habits
   B distinctive plumages of male and female
   C a common aid to identifying each type of duck
   D the reasons why ducks migrate
   E ducks' nesting habits

From Section B

9 Which ONE of the following is closest in meaning to 'disport themselves' in l. 3?

   A court the opposite sex
   B feel enjoyment
   C perform acrobatics
   D amuse themselves
   E find relaxation

10 To 'culminate in' (l. 7) means to

   A reach their highest point in
   B find their termination in
   C take the form of
   D create as a consequence
   E lead up to

11 Which ONE of the following remarks is most true about the paragraph ll. 1–30?

   A it preserves its unity because it includes a series of examples of how ducks think and behave
   B it progresses from the pleasant characteristics of ducks to the unpleasant ones
   C it deals with four quite different topics: ducks' love of play, their use of 'baby-sitters', their ability to think, and their spitefulness
   D it deals entirely with the author's own observations of ducks
   E it concentrates consistently on the types of ingenuity shown by ducks

12 Wigeon are appropriately called 'opportunists' (l. 24) because they

   A allow due weight to circumstances in choosing their strategy
   B seize the advantages that chance offers them
   C prefer what can be done to what should be done

D try to curry favour with more powerful birds

E adopt different feeding-habits at different times of the year

13 Which ONE of the following is closest in meaning to 'sedulous' as used in l. 25?

A cowardly

B painstaking

C opportunist

D flattering

E parasitic

14 Which ONE of the following is closest in meaning to 'protuberance' in l. 42?

A prominent feature

B point

C swelling

D bulge

E pinnacle

15 A 'spatulate' bill (l. 45) means one that is

A flattened

B narrow

C slender

D characteristic

E broad

From Section C

16 Ducks are difficult to observe because they

A usually retreat to quiet, secluded places

B usually position themselves so that the light falls inconveniently for bird-watchers

C are quickly scared if you look at them through field-glasses

D easily take fright when a bird-watcher finds their more secluded haunts

E seem to appear only when the sun shines

17 Which ONE of the following is closest in meaning to 'congregate' in l. 5?

A migrate to a different area

B divide themselves into different species

C come together in a crowd

D mix with different species

E act almost like worshippers (of nature)

18 'Enthralling' (l. 19) means

A habit-forming

B fascinating

C engrossing

    D intensifying
    E relaxing

19 The author does not really complete the arguments of ll. 22–8. But presumably he means that people who shoot duck
    A take care that the right numbers are allowed to breed
    B include some of the author's closest friends
    C forget, while they are shooting, that they love to see duck
    D do not care whether other people in addition to themselves ever see ducks
    E regard mere bird-watching as too tame a pastime

20 Which ONE of the following remarks about punctuation is *not* correct?
    A the dash in l. 6 shows that the rest of the sentence is a casual after-thought
    B the colon in l. 11 introduces an addition that explains what has gone before
    C the commas before and after 'however' in l. 15 are used to bracket off a sentence adverb.
    D the semi-colon in l. 14 emphasizes the contrast between using a telescope and using field-glasses
    E the comma in l. 16 divides what are two distinctly separate ideas

21 The statement that most accurately sums up the whole of Section C is:
    A it is surprisingly easy to see ducks near large towns
    B it is rarely easy to see big flocks of duck without a telescope
    C there is both difficulty and fascination in watching ducks
    D one is more likely to forget the discomforts of watching ducks if one can identify different species
    E it is possible both to enjoy watching duck and to enjoy shooting them

TRADITIONAL QUESTIONS

Answer the following questions in your own words as far as possible. Questions marked with an asterisk should be answered *very briefly*, and in these answers complete sentences are not necessary.

From Section A

    *1 Give in a single word or short phrase the meaning of *four* of the following words *as used in the passage*:
        i inconspicuous (l. 10)   **ii** moult (l. 17)   **iii** distinctive (l. 21)
        iv identification (l. 24)   **v** ornithologists (l. 35).

    2 What are the two categories of ducks mentioned in paragraph 1? What differences are there between them?

    3 How does the plumage of the Sheld-duck differ from that of most species of northern ducks? Why?

4 Why is the word 'eclipse' (l. 17) in inverted commas? Explain the meaning of the word as used here.

5 What is the difference, according to the writer, between the habits of ganders and drakes?

6 What does the metaphor 'colonies' (l. 33) convey that a plain statement would lack?

From Section B

*7 Give in a single word or short phrase the meaning of *five* of the following words *as used in the passage*:

i culminate (l. 7) ii complicated (l. 10) iii opportunists (l. 24)
iv sedulous (l. 25) v succulent (l. 26) vi harry (l. 28).

8 'The psychology of ducks is a study with great possibilities.' (l. 1).
In about 80 of your own words show how, according to the writer, ducks have powers of thought and reasoning.

9 Why do ducks lay large numbers of eggs?

10 Explain what is meant by the expression 'to pool their families' (l. 12).

From Section C

*11 Give in a single word or short phrase the meaning of the following words *as used in the passage*:

i characteristic (l. 16) ii bunched (l. 17) iii countered (l. 18)
iv enthralling (l. 19).

12 Explain the expression 'to take the more easy line' (l. 4).

13 What, according to the writer, are the difficulties of watching duck 'in the truly wild state' (ll. 9–10)?

14 What is the paradox near the end of Section C?

II. Writing English

Write on ONE of the following:

a An experience, frightening or amusing, which occurred while you were engaged in an outdoor hobby or occupation.
b An expedition, by sea or land, to study some aspect of animal or plant life.
c Falconry.
d The problems of people living in 'high-rise' blocks of flats.

e   'O nuclear wind, when wilt thou blow
         That the small rain down can rain?
         Christ, that my love were in my arms
         And I had my arms again.'

Discuss the continued testing of nuclear bombs.

f Fashion. You might consider the absurdities of some fashions, the reasons why women—and men—discard almost new clothes in favour of
   the latest styles, the harm some extreme fashions can cause—for
   example, in footwear.

g Write a story, a description or an essay suggested by the illustration
   above. (Your composition may be directly about the subject of the il-

lustration, or may only take suggestions from it, but there must be some clear connection between the illustration and the composition.)

Suggestions for Projects, Assignments and Course Work

1 The history of the motor-cycle.
2 Cookery through the ages.
3 Butterflies and moths.

III. Using English

Punctuation

1 You have arrived late for school OR an appointment OR an interview. Construct the dialogue between your teacher or the person you should have met and you. Use direct speech and be careful to punctuate accurately. You should write about 200 words and don't forget to apologize if you feel it is necessary.

2 Correct the punctuation of the following sentences, giving reasons for your changes.

i There was a bright moon but it was behind the clouds, it was a fine dry night but it was uncommonly dark, paths, hedges, fields, houses and trees were enveloped, in one deep shade. ii The judge asked whether there were any more witnesses? iii The Marquis of Granby in Mrs. Wellers time was a model of a roadside public house of the better class. Just large enough to be convenient and small enough to be snug.

3 Account for the following marks of punctuation in the passage in Part I:

i the commas after 'ganders' (l.A. 13) and after 'parents' (l.A. 14)
ii the commas after 'Mallard', 'Teal', and 'Wigeon' (l.A. 26)
iii the commas before and after 'often in large numbers' (l.A. 34)
iv the semi-colon after 'problem' (l.B. 21) v the colon after 'wrong' (l.C. 11).

Grammar and Usage

4 Explain the meaning of the following expressions by any method you choose:

i to let the cat out of the bag ii to smell a rat iii let sleeping dogs lie iv a black sheep v to put the cart before the horse.

5 Use the following words in separate sentences to show you understand their meaning:

i intrinsic ii credulous iii hibernate iv sceptical v unanimous vi mutual.

Spelling and Dictionary Work

6 Find out the derivation of the following words:

i smog ii moped iii portfolio iv porpoise v kindergarten
vi vamp vii cyclone viii orang-outang ix foolscap
x blancmange.

7 The following words are incomplete. The dots indicate a letter or letters missing. The number of the dots bears no relationship to the number of letters missing. Write down the words, spelling them correctly.

i monast.... y ii doct.... r iii peac.... ble
iv chang.... ble v instr.... ment vi practi.... e (verb)
vii parl.... ment viii hyg.... nic ix succes.... ul
x maint.... nance.

Style and Appreciation

8 The following extract is taken from *A Sound of Thunder* by Ray Bradbury.

'It came on great oiled, resilient, striding legs. It towered thirty feet above half of the trees, a great evil god, folding its delicate watchmaker's claws close to its oily reptilian chest. Each lower leg was a piston, a thousand pounds of white bone, sunk in thick ropes of muscle, sheathed over in a gleam of pebbled skin like the mail of a terrible warrior. Each thigh was a ton of meat, ivory, and steel mesh. And from the great breathing cage of the upper body those two delicate arms dangled out front, arms with hands which might pick up and examine men like toys, while the snake neck coiled. And the head itself, a ton of sculptured stone, lifted easily upon the sky. Its mouth gaped, exposing a fence of teeth like daggers. Its eyes rolled, ostrich eggs, empty of all expression save hunger. It closed its mouth in a death grin. It ran, its pelvic bones crushing aside trees and bushes, its taloned feet clawing damp earth, leaving prints six inches deep wherever it settled its weight. It ran with a gliding ballet step, far too poised and balanced for its ten tons. It moved into a sunlit arena warily, its beautifully reptile hands feeling the air.'

This is a description of *Tyrannosaurus Rex*. What qualities does the writer emphasize, and how does he do it? Note particularly the use of metaphor, simile and choice of adjectives.

Books to read

Zoo Quest for a Dragon	David Attenborough
The Ascent of Everest	Sir John Hunt
Three Singles to Adventure	Gerald Durrell
The Herries Chronicles	Hugh Walpole
Wuthering Heights	Emily Brontë
A Fall of Moondust	Arthur C. Clarke
The Guns of Navarone	Alistair Maclean
Connoisseur's Science Fiction	ed. T. Boardman
The Seeds of Time	John Wyndham
The Kon-Tiki Expedition	Thor Heyerdahl

Unit 14

I. Reading and Understanding

Read the following passage (which for your convenience has been divided into three sections) and then answer the questions.

THE CHARM OF CRICKET

[A]   A collection of score cards faded with age, a volume of *Wisden* yellow as autumn sunshine, will speak of the English climate and of the English summer's caprices. The hot days witness the processional movement of batsmen to their centuries; the wet days see them dispossessed, disenthroned, and of no account. The weather of England enters cricket like a *deus ex machina*. On a warm Sabbath afternoon, brilliant with sunshine, following a thunderstorm at church-time, I was walking in Hyde Park when I met two famous Yorkshiremen—Wilfred Rhodes and Emmott Robinson. Yorkshire had batted at Lord's throughout Saturday and had scored nearly four hundred runs.

'It's cleared up nicely,' I said to the two old soldiers of Yorkshire as I greeted them. Emmott nearly snapped my head off.

'Aye!' he retorted, like a knife, 'and a sticky wicket going' to wa-aste at Loards!' It was an attack on unnecessary Seventh Day observance.

There are better games, as games. Frequently there is no decision at all in cricket, sometimes scarcely a beginning. But it is on rainy days that the charm of the game has been known to work its most subtle spells for those who play county cricket. The vacant and rural field is shrouded in mist as you walk through the entrance-gate hoping against hope. There is a sound of footsteps on the wooden pavilion; perhaps there'll be play after all. Then the clouds are suddenly pulled apart, and the sun changes the grass to a field of jewels. And men in white appear from nowhere, and soon two little mounds of sawdust are placed at each end of the wicket and bowlers sometimes lose volition like boys on a slide, and the bat sends forth its ineffectual thud; while in adjacent trees the birds make busy noises, and aloft in the blue sky there are great castles on cliffs of clouds, and burning lakes. These things all belong to the game as much as the implements, the technical achievement, and the 'result'.

The foreigner is naturally baffled. He arrives in London and sees a newspaper poster: 'England's Danger'. An international crisis has occurred behind his back, during his journey from the   35 Continent! No; but almost as important, six wickets have fallen at Lord's to the invading Australians.

Any savant examining *a priori* the evolution of cricket could easily fall into far-reaching fallacies. The shape of the bat, to begin with—in the early days when cricket was mixed up with other of   40 the nation's field-sports, and was patronized by the Fancy and went hand-in-hand with cock-fighting and gambling—in those bad old times, the cricket bat was crooked in shape, or at least it was curved. But in the high noon of Victorian respectability, after muscular Christians had incorporated the game into the curricu-   45 lum of an English gentleman's education, why, by this time the bat was straight and of white willow made. Two sayings became liturgical almost, 'Play a Straight Bat', and 'It's not Cricket'.

[B]   It is far more than a game, this cricket. It somehow holds the mirror up to English nature. We are no hypocrites, but we try to make the best of things of contrary appeal. It was once alleged that W. G. Grace now and again cheated. I asked an old Glouces-tershire 'pro' to speak frankly on this subject. 'Nay!' he protested   5 with proud emphasis, 'never. The "Old Man" cheat?—'e were too clever for that.' We are expedient as a people, and not without humour. The history of cricket, made by Englishmen no more ethical than jockeys and pugilists and footballers, does justice like a play or a pageant to our national horse-sense, sentiment, and   10 powers of accommodation.

The crooked bat became straight out of sheer expediency: wit and not morality was the cause. A curved bat, with the weight concentrated at the bottom, was necessary as a counter to the ancient underhand bowling, quick and along the ground, almost 'grubs'.   15 As soon as Hambledon men bowled a length and used the air and caused the ball to rise sharply from the ground, a hockey-stick sort of defence was of no avail, and so the shouldered narrow blade was evolved. Even this most hallowed of symbols of cricket, the straight bat, was not given its fair and narrowish rectitude by   20 some categorical imperative issued from conscience and ethic; oh dear no! In the beginning no bound was put by law on the width of a blade. One day a cricketer of Reigate came into action with a bat broader than the wicket. Alas for the vision that overreacheth, a rule was brought in enforcing a four-and-a-half inch limit. None   25 the less, the Archimedes of Reigate—'Shock' White to his intimate friends—had his hour and it became immortal.

Three stumps pointing heavenward from the earth!—our
savant would deduce from the first sight of them some show of
Trinitarianism, especially in view of the large number of the clergy   30
present at any cricket match on the field and off. But once again,
the truth, the pragmatical truth, has to be confessed: the three
wickets came into use only by the exigency that drives all of us,
saints and sinners alike. In the Maytime of 1775 a fierce engagement took place between five men of Hambledon and five men of   35
Kent. When the last man went in, fourteen runs were wanted for a
Hambledon victory. 'Lumpy' Stevens, who was playing for Kent
as a 'given man,' bowled through the wicket defended by John
Small—and the point is that the wicket then consisted of only two
stumps with one bail like the crossbar of a gate. The frustration of   40
'Lumpy', as he beat John Small's bat time after time and saw the
ball go vainly through the wicket, must have been awful and elo-
quently expressed, not only there and then but for long afterwards; for a third stump was added two years afterwards.

[C]   It is because cricket does not always hurry along, a constant
hurly-burly, every player propelled here and there by the pace of
continuous action, that there is time for character to reveal itself.
We remember not the scores and the results in after years; it is the
men who remain in our minds, in our imagination. Nobody asks   5
what was the batting average of Joseph Guy, a Nottinghamshire
cricketer of whom it was said that he was 'elegance, all elegance,
fit to play before the Queen in her parlour'.
    We do not know, and we are not curious about, the bowling
averages of 'Lumpy' Stevens, who rose early on summer mornings   10
at Hambledon to pick a wicket; for in those days the spin of a coin
decided not only first innings but also gave the winner the right to
choose the pitch. 'Lumpy' loved to send fast 'shooters', and he invariably chose a wicket with a downward slope—'for honest
"Lumpy" did allow, He ne'er could pitch but o'er a brow'. Lineal   15
descendants of 'Lumpy' were Emmott Robinson and Rhodes,
who once inspected the wicket at Leeds after a wet morning. The
sun was shining just before lunch, and Rhodes and Emmott
pressed expert fingers into the texture of the turf. 'It'll be "sticky"
at four o'clock,' said Rhodes. Emmott pressed and fondled the   20
turf again, then answered: 'No, Wilfred, half-past.'
    The state of the turf is the clue to every cricket match; no other
game comes as much under the influence of material circumstances; the elements are cricket's presiding geniuses.
    Not until we have considered the material conditions and en-   25
vironment of cricket—which include the implements, especially

the heavy roller—can we measure exponent with exponent and period with period. Of the early Hambledon epoch we must be content to savour the character and the spirit; for technically the Hambledon game is scarcely linked even to the cricket of only fifty 30 years afterwards. Hambledon men, as we know, bowled underarm; it was later than Hambledon, in May, 1828, when the MCC legalized the round-arm action. The 'new' bowling became the rage at once; and a Sussex team, with Lillywhite in it, used round-arms so drastically that they thrashed All England twice in three 35 matches.

NEVILLE CARDUS, English Cricket (Collins)

NOTE: *Wisden* is an annual magazine giving information about cricket. Wilfred Rhodes and Emmott Robinson were successful batsmen and bowlers for Yorkshire in the period before and after the 1914–18 war. Dr W. G. Grace is still thought of as the greatest cricketer of all time. Hambledon in Hampshire, if not the 'cradle' of cricket, was the home of the game in its infancy and vigorous youth.

MULTIPLE CHOICE QUESTIONS

After reading each of the following questions, choose the ONE correct answer, and indicate it by writing down the letter that stands for it.

From Section A

1 The first paragraph (ll. 1–11) stresses that the characteristic appeal of cricket lies in its

    A dependence on changes of the weather
    B ability to remind us of the past
    C production of interesting personalities such as Rhodes
    D appeal to the eye of the spectator
    E reminders of warm summers in the past

2 Emmott Robinson (ll. 12–14) is angry because

    A the weather would have helped him to score runs if the game had been played on the Sunday
    B Cardus supports Yorkshire's opponents
    C he regards Cardus as rather a chatterbox
    D the weather has produced a bowler's wicket when he cannot bowl
    E he believes that cricket should be played regularly on Sundays

3 The thud of the bat is ineffectual (l. 28) because

    A the batsman cannot score so easily on a wet out-field
    B Cardus is describing a time when bats were curved rather than straight

    C the team that is batting is likely to lose the game

    D the spectators are surprised to hear the noise of ball on bat

    E it is not as loud as the songs of the birds

4 The main idea of the paragraph (ll. 17–32) beginning 'There are better games' is that

    A unexpected pleasures are preferable to expected ones

    B cricket is more interesting when played on a wet wicket

    C the surroundings and circumstances are an important part of the charm of cricket

    D a village cricket game will have a surprising result when it follows a sudden improvement in the weather

    E cricket would be a better game if there was always a definite result

5 Which ONE of the following remarks about comparisons is not true?

    A in l. 2 the yellow colour of an old copy of Wisden is compared to the yellow sunshine of an autumn day

    B in l. 5 batsmen on a wet day are compared to kings who have lost their power

    C in l. 14 the speed and severity of Emmott Robinson's answer is compared to the speed and sharpness of a knife

    D in ll. 24–5 the sun shining on wet grass makes it sparkle like precious stones

    E in l. 33 the astonishment of the foreigner is compared to that of a person confused by having to listen to several noises simultaneously

6 'England's Danger' (l. 34) refers only to a cricket match: this seems to Cardus to be

    A typically English

    B showing a loss of real values

    C journalistically conventional

    D completely misleading

    E stylistically puzzling to a foreigner

7 The sentence 'An international crisis has occurred behind his back, during his journey from the Continent' (ll. 34–6).

    A suggests that the foreign visitor panics unnecessarily about politics

    B explains what the foreigner imagines has happened

    C explains the true reason for the foreigner's surprise

    D stresses the differences between Englishmen and foreigners

    E ironically states the opposite of the truth

8 'Fallacies' (l. 39) are

    A errors in reasoning

    B wild exaggerations

    C unusual mistakes

    D attempts to split hairs

    E debating points

9 The phrase to 'play a straight bat' (l. 48) arose in the days when

   A batsmanship become more of a science

   B cricket was popular with aristocrats who enjoyed watching boxing and cock-fighting

   C the curriculum of public schools was being reformed

   D the decisive influence on the game was being exercised by amateurs

   E Victorian Christians thought that cricket encouraged a moral attitude to life

10 Which ONE of the following ideas would you *omit* if you were summarizing the main points that are actually made in Section A?

   A a collection of old books records weather statistics for past years

   B decisive events in past cricket matches often depended on the weather

   C Rhodes and Robinson were once angry that rain produced a perfect wicket for bowlers—on a Sunday

   D wonderful cricket matches often follow a wet morning

   E the Victorians literally adopted a straight bat and metaphorically admired what it came to stand for

From Section B

11 In writing about W. G. Grace (ll. 3–7) Cardus does not paint him as an innocent amateur; instead he suggests that

   A it was sporting to do certain things not forbidden by the rules

   B cricketers are entitled to do what the rules do not openly forbid

   C Grace was not a typical cricketer

   D professionalism has spoiled the game since W. G. Grace's day

   E W. G. Grace tried to have the best of both worlds

12 'It somehow holds the mirror up to English nature' (ll. 1–2) means that cricket

   A shows up the faults of those who take part in it

   B reveals the character of those who play it

   C encourages players to stop just short of cheating

   D gives a distorted picture of the Englishman's nature

   E gives players a clearer picture of their own motives

13 'Ethical' (l. 9) describes people who are

   A uninterested in money

   B clever in a professional way

   C aware of what is right and wrong

   D playing games for money

   E concerned with religion

14 The phrase 'powers of accommodation' (l. 11) means ability to

   A agree with both sides

   B change the rules to suit ourselves

C adjust our morality to what is possible
D keep to what is relevant
E maintain a sense of right and wrong

15 'Even this . . . . ethic' (ll. 19–21) means that the straight bat
A reflected and symbolized early cricketers' views on morality
B was nearly laughed out of existence by a joking batsman
C did not have the moral aspect that was claimed
D taught cricketers the importance of playing fair
E was not made compulsory by new laws of cricket

16 'Alas for the vision that overreacheth' (l. 24) suggests that 'Shock' White from Reigate
A had a longer reach than most batsmen
B exploited the vagueness of the law too ruthlessly to be forgiven
C was too ambitious to have a chance of getting away with his action
D was holding the game up to ridicule
E is nowadays thought to have acted unfairly

17 The essential point of paragraph 2 (ll. 12–27) is that the modern shape of the bat
A was evolved as a symbol of fair sportsmanship
B was necessary to deal with grubbers
C was intended to give the bowler a fair chance
D developed when bowlers achieved more bounce
E illustrates the moral nature of the game of cricket

18 'Exigency' (l. 33) means
A circumstances that compel us to act in one way
B an emergency that arose unexpectedly
C the requirement that certain things must be done
D the eagerness to introduce changes
E a guide to moral and sporting behaviour

19 Cardus stresses how often the ball passed through the two wickets defended by John Small (ll. 41–2) in order to
A illustrate the decisiveness of chance in deciding games of cricket
B show how accurate a bowler 'Lumpy' Stevens was
C explain why two wickets were replaced by three
D include an example from the cricket of the past
E stress how angry 'Lumpy' Stevens felt

20 The essential point of the paragraph 3 (ll. 28–44) is that
A the rules of cricket in the Hambledon period were very different from today's
B 'Lumpy' Stevens easily lost his temper when he could not get a batsman out

    C when once 'Lumpy' Stevens began to grumble he went on grumbling till he got things changed

    D a third stump was made necessary by the chanciness of needing to hit two stumps

    E the three stumps represented the three persons in the Trinity

From Section C

21 The central idea of ll. 1–8 is that cricket

    A includes pauses in the activity of the players

    B is played at a slow pace

    C encourages players to show their individual characters

    D makes us interested in averages and records

    E appeals to enthusiasts' imagination.

22 Cardus stresses that Stevens, Rhodes and Robinson shared

    A their determination to use the rules to their advantage

    B the ability to get up early in the morning

    C a love of their native counties

    D an expert knowledge of turf wickets

    E the same resolute determination to win

23 The elements are 'cricket's presiding genius' (l. 24) because the

    A state of the light makes a great difference to batting

    B effect of the weather on the wicket is decisive

    C game depends on its success in producing brilliant star players

    D history of cricket reflects economic and social changes

    E type of cricket played by Hambledon men was very different from the modern game

TRADITIONAL QUESTIONS

Answer the following questions in your own words as far as possible. Questions marked with an asterisk should be answered *very briefly*, and in these answers complete sentences are not necessary.

From Section A

  *1 Give in a single word or short phrase the meaning of *five* of the following words *as used in the passage*:

    i caprices (l. 3) **ii** subtle (l. 20) **iii** baffled (l. 33) **iv** fallacies (l. 39)

    v curriculum (l. 45) **vi** liturgical (l. 47).

  2 Pick out and comment on one example of each of the following from this section:

    i simile **ii** metaphor **iii** personification.

  3 Explain the meaning of the following:

    i 'patronized by the Fancy' (l. 41) **ii** 'went hand in hand with cock-fighting and gambling' (l. 42).

4 The author admits that cricket as a game has its drawbacks. Name TWO of them.

5 Quote THREE expressions from this section to show that the writer places cricket far above other sports.

From Section B

*6 Give in a single word or short phrase the meaning of *four* of the following words *as used in the passage*:
i expediency (l. 12) ii hallowed (l. 19) iii immortal (l. 27)
iv engagement (l. 34) v frustration (l. 40).

7 What does the writer mean by saying that cricket 'holds the mirror up to English nature' (ll. 1–2)? Choose TWO examples which Cardus uses to support this statement and show how they do it.

8 Why does the writer call the straight bat a symbol of cricket (ll. 19–20)?

9 In about thirty of your own words say why the 'crooked' bat became 'straight'.

10 Why does the writer call 'Shock' White the 'Archimedes of Reigate' (l. 26)?

11 Explain in about thirty of your own words why the wicket was increased from two to three stumps.

12 Explain briefly the meaning of:
i 'powers of accommodation' (l. 11) ii 'wit and not morality was the cause' (ll. 12–13) iii 'Alas for the vision that overreacheth' (l. 24).

From Section C

*13 Give in a single word or short phrase the meaning of FOUR of the following words *as used in the passage:*
i hurly-burly (l. 2) ii exponent (l. 27) iii savour (l. 29)
iv technically (l. 29) v rage (l. 34).

14 What is the meaning of 'the Hambledon game is scarcely linked even to the cricket of only fifty years afterwards' (ll. 29–31)?

15 Put into your own words 'the elements are cricket's presiding geniuses' (l. 24).

16 How fully or successfully does Cardus prove his main argument —that 'no other game comes so much under the influence of material circumstances' (ll. 22–4).

II. Writing English

Write on ONE of the following:

a Your favourite sport. Indicate its particular attraction for you, illustrating your remarks with short stories of incidents you have experienced or witnessed. Introduce characters, players or spectators, and use (not too much) suitable dialogue.

b Do 'national sports' reflect the character of nations? Consider such sports as baseball, cricket, football, and bullfighting, which might be called 'national'.

c You have heard of the 'Generation Gap'. Show how it affects your life and family.

d Write a composition on what is suggested to you by the following lines:

> Let's say good-bye to hedges
> And roads with grassy edges
>   And winding country lanes;
> Let all things travel faster
> Where motor-car is master
>   Till only Speed remains.
>
> When all our roads are lighted
> By concrete monsters sited
>   Like gallows overhead,
> Bathed in the yellow vomit
> Each monster belches from it,
>   We'll know that we are dead.

JOHN BETJEMAN, *Inexpensive Progress* (John Murray)

e The view from the bridge.

f The spectator sees most of the game, especially if he watches it on television!

g Write TWO short compositions chosen from the following:

  i A character sketch of one of your friends or relations
  ii Looking after pets
  iii Neighbours
  iv The scene at a supermarket.

Suggestions for Projects. Assignments and Course Work

1 Choose a district, region or county. Read all the articles, poems and books you can find which deal with the area you have chosen. Describe its character from what you have seen and/or read. You can deal broadly with your subject, or with some particular aspect, such as its history, flora, fauna, industries, folk-lore etc.

2 Choose an important historical event which took place in the area where you are living, for example the murder of Becket for those living in Kent, the Battle of Hastings for those in Sussex, the Great Fire of London for those in that area. Produce an edition of the local newspaper that would have been published immediately after this event if modern newspapers had existed then. Your paper should include, in addition to the news of the important event, all the usual local items of interest, including advertisements and illustrations.

III Using English

Punctuation

1 Account for the following marks of punctuation in the passage in Part I:

i the semi-colon after 'centuries' (l.A. 4) ii the dash after 'Yorkshireman' (l.A. 9) iii the inverted commas before and after 'Play a Straight Bat' (l.A. 48) iv the commas after 'horse-sense' and 'sentiment' (l.B. 10) v the colon after 'expediency' (l.B. 12) vi the comma after 'ground' (l.B. 15) vii the dash before 'Shock White' (l.B. 26) and after 'friends' (l.B. 27) viii the colon after 'confessed' (l.B. 32) ix the inverted commas before and after 'sticky' (l.C. 19) x the commas before and after 'Wilfred' (l.C. 21).

2 Punctuate and improve the wording of the following

i When he jumped the barrier fell down ii The servant said his master was cruel iii Until they moved their television was useless iv Please return books wanted urgently (telegram).

Grammar and Usage

3 What part of speech is 'score' (l.A. 1)? Use this word in separate sentences as two other parts of speech (two sentences).

4 Use the word 'sound' in three separate sentences as noun, adjective, and verb.

5 Pick out one example each of a proper noun, a common noun, a collective noun, and an abstract noun from the passage in Part I.

Spelling and Dictionary Work

6 Single and double 'l'.

1 quarrel—quarrelling, quarreller, quarrelled; compel—compelling, compeller, compelled.
2 roll—rolling, roller, rolled; pull—pulling, puller, pulled.
3 all—altogether, already.
4 +full—helpful; beautiful.
Although there are exceptions (as in almost all 'rules' of English spelling) the above examples should help. Study them and try to compile your own rules for the single or double 'l'.

7 From your dictionary find the meanings of the expressions *deus ex machina* (l.A. 6) and *a priori* (l.A. 38).

8 Use your dictionary to find out why the writer uses the word 'Trinitarianism' (l.B. 30).

9 Use the following in separate sentences to show the difference in meaning between the words in the following pairs:

i theirs, there's **ii** its, it's **iii** whose, who's **iv** your, you're
v wont, won't.

Style and Appreciation

10 Pick out all the expressions from the passage in Part I which the writer uses to stress the importance and seriousness of cricket.

11 What are the main qualities of the writer's style? Show how he varies his style to suit the subject matter.

12
> 'Dawn's cold imperative compels
> Bazaars and gutters to disturb
> Famine's casual ugly tableaux.'

These are the first three lines of a poem called 'Indian Day' by Alun Lewis. Try to express the ideas in your own words. Notice how condensed the poet's thought is, and how this is due to the use of figurative language. Try to explain the figurative expressions as shown in Paper 1, Part III, (6).

Books to read

Memoirs of a Fox-Hunting Man	Siegfried Sassoon
Cricket Country	Edmund Blunden
The Catcher in the Rye	J. D. Salinger
Cider with Rosie	Laurie Lee
English Journey	J. B. Priestley
The Loneliness of the Long Distance Runner	Alan Sillitoe
The Lost World	A. Conan Doyle
The Illustrated Man	Ray Bradbury
Jamaica Inn	Daphne du Maurier
The African Queen	C. S. Forester

Unit 15

I. Reading and Understanding

Read the following passage (which for your convenience has been divided into three sections) and then answer the questions.

THE NEW ENTHUSIASM FOR RAILWAYS

[A]   Although railways have formed part of our civilization for nearly a century and a half it is only in recent years that large numbers of people have taken more than a passing interest in their operation and development. There have always been railway enthusiasts, both amateur and professional, but these have greatly   5
increased in numbers and depth of technical knowledge since the Second World War, especially during the past ten or twelve years.

By a strange paradox this new interest in railways lies parallel to their decline as a major form of public transport. It is only since the challenge of motorways, for both passenger and goods ser-   10
vices, that preservation schemes have been launched, popular visits organized to railway installations and not even a remote branch line allowed to close without public ceremonies, television interviews and serious letters or articles appearing in the press. It is only during the second half of the twentieth century that trips   15
have been arranged for railway enthusiasts taking them as far afield as South Africa, India, North America and Australia. More books are written on transport in general and railways in particular than on any other subject, while collecting and operating model railways has become one of the most popular indoor hob-   20
bies in the world.

At first the enthusiasm of a second 'railway mania' may seem little more than nostalgic and sentimental. The more advanced nations and cultures of the west have always tended to regret their past, especially during times of transition when there is a genuine   25
danger of losing contact with former environment. Yet while to record and preserve something of the past may be described as either a duty or a luxury—according to outlook—it is seldom that such matters lie within the scope of ordinary individuals or those of average means. While historic buildings, valuable paintings   30
and tapestries are the preserve of public bodies or persons of ample wealth, the collection of many items of railwayana lies open

to the majority—from the schoolboy collecting tickets at pocket
money prices to those wishing to acquire a locomotive, items of
rolling stock, signalling equipment or even a complete railway sta-   35
tion.

The future of railways and their economics are beyond the
scope of these chapters. There are heartening signs, however, that
modernization and increased efficiency may win back custom
from both roads and airways in the not too distant future. Prom-   40
ised schedules of 130 m.p.h. and upwards between the larger
cities—centre to centre—may open the second great era of rail
transport, no less exciting than the boom of the mid-nineteenth
century. Yet it is keeping the railways efficient and up to the
minute that helps to bring so many interesting relics before the   45
public. Even British Railways have finally recognized the importance of railwayana and objects formerly scrapped or discarded
are now preserved in transport museums or offered to the enthusiast at reasonable prices.

Historians are now increasingly aware of the importance of   50
transport studies in understanding the development of civilization. From this viewpoint alone a valid and not unattractive case
may be made for the preservation of both railways and railway
relics. Yet this is only one explanation of a complex subject. The
need and interest to collect things of personal value lies beyond   55
reasonable analysis. In the case of railwayana it is a mystery
equalled only by the magic of railways themselves, finding devotees in all parts of the world. All that may be needed to start a collection are modest funds and storage space. Background
knowledge may be acquired both in practice and by reading   60
numerous books and magazine articles on railway subjects.

[B]   As with most forms of collecting this aspect of railwayana
needs both definite aims and careful selection. It is rarely possible,
however, to be highly specialized in the early stages. Most people
start with a piecemeal assortment, vaguely concerned with railways, lacking both coherence and more than personal interest.   5
Yet as the enthusiasm grows there is also a tendency to cull out
less valuable objects and search for items of particular significance. In this way the collector is eventually faced with a pattern
of development clearly defined by objectives and limitations.

Many of the more obvious limitations concern the amount of   10
money to be spent and space available for either storage or display. There are also limitations of size as locomotive nameplates
and some of the larger items require a more spacious setting than a
'bed-sitter' or even the lounge of a small suburban house. It is

ideal to have a converted garden shed, loft or unwanted garage   15
space for the display of many larger objects—with the use of a
work bench for cleaning and restoration purposes. Perhaps the
most fortunate in this respect are those with the older type
house—retaining a small stable block or range of outbuildings.

Items displayed in average-sized living-rooms are, of necessity,   20
much smaller than those collected by enthusiasts for whom space
is no object. In many cases they are of considerable interest from
viewpoints of decor and ornament. Skilfully displayed items on a
railway theme, including model railway equipment, have often
proved ideal background material for club room, bar or res-   25
taurant, especially where fellow enthusiasts are likely to meet. It
may be noted, however, that most items are heavy for their size
and should be firmly secured to supporting base, background or
wall surface.

[C]   The model railway hobby has undergone an unexpected
renaissance during the past decade, and now includes large numbers of people who not only operate and construct their own
layouts, but who collect both toy trains and elaborate scale
models.   5

To the average enthusiast scale models are sure to have an
obvious appeal, forming an extension to the collection of lamps,
name-plates and other items in the round. A finely modelled locomotive in a glass case is an enviable acquisition in any household
and, judging by recent trends, may soon challenge the model gal-   10
leon or clipper as an accepted item of decorative interest.

While many people would be able to appreciate the craftsmanship and decorative appeal of a scale model it is perhaps less
easy to define an enthusiasm for old tinplate engines and railway
accessories. With many collectors of model railways and toy   15
trains buying a few odds and ends is frequently the prelude to
operations. While a model locomotive is charming enough on the
shelf even the least curious may feel an urge to see the motions
work and the wheels go round. Models intended for work are
usually of greater value if advertised in working order, which   20
naturally leads to a simple test track on a portable baseboard,
leading—in the course of time—to a permanent branch line in the
loft or an experimental layout through the rock garden.

Model railways are certainly an interesting hobby, by any standards, involving a wide range of artistic, craft and mechanical   25
skills. Their varied scales and gauges range from the near micro-
scopic to passenger-carrying equipment more correctly termed
miniature railways. The first models produced on a commercial

scale were mainly imported into Britain from Germany during the
second half of the nineteenth century. They were stocked, during   30
the early winter months, in the unlikely windows of chemists and
haberdashers, and were given to mechanically minded boys as
Christmas presents. W. J. Bassett-Lowke, formerly the doyen of
British model railways, was apprenticed to the family engineering
works in Northampton during the 1890s, but was already making   35
a profitable sideline out of scale fittings and components for the
increasing number of serious modellers. After visiting a continental trade exhibition and making contacts with several foreign
manufacturers he decided to develop the potential of the home
market by making and selling a complete railway system designed   40
by himself or his assistants from authentic British prototypes.
Bassett-Lowke models became a household name and were familiar in thousands of British homes for over fifty years. Whilst Bassett-Lowke sold a number of excellent models—made to the
highest possible standards—the most typical of the Bassett-   45
Lowke products were in the medium price range offering character and performance allied to strength and durability. Compared
with both earlier and later models, either functioning correctly
but looking atrocious or performing badly while appearing immaculate, Bassett-Lowke offered not so much a compromise but a   50
solution.

DONALD J. SMITH, *Discovering Railwayana* (Shire Publications)

MULTIPLE CHOICE QUESTIONS

After reading each of the following questions, choose the ONE correct
answer, and indicate it by writing down the letter that stands for it.

From Section A

1 Which ONE of the following best sums up Section A as a whole?

   A it is probable that the introduction of high speed trains between
cities will lead to an expansion in rail traffic

   B at the very time when the survival of railways is threatened, more
people have become interested in their past

   C the desire to preserve parts of past railways is fundamentally due to
sentimental reasons

   D the history of a modern country can be best understood by studying the development of its railways

   E the fascinating relics of our railways can best be preserved by individuals

2 If you were summarizing separately the four main ideas of Section A,
which ONE of the following would you omit?

A just when the existence of railways has been threatened, more people have become fascinated by them

B at first this new enthusiasm to preserve railways and things connected with them may seem sentimental

C the new modernization of railways, which may bring back traffic to them, is increasing the number of enthusiasts

D it is more important to modernize the railways than to preserve relics of their past

E British Railways, historians and private collectors all should play an essential part in preserving part of the railways' past

3 Which TWO of the following form the essential parts of the 'paradox' referred to in l. 8?

  i an increased interest in railways
  ii protests against the closing of branch lines
  iii a reduction in rail traffic
  iv the writing of more and more books about railways

A i and ii only
B i and iii only
C i and iv only
D ii and iii only
E iii and iv only

4 'nostalgic' (l. 23) means

A lacking in realism
B longing with wistful melancholy for the past
C ignoring economic considerations
D keen to the point of fanaticism
E based on expert knowledge

5 Which TWO of the following sentences form asides, not essential to the main argument?

  i 'At first . . . . . . sentimental' (ll. 22–3)
  ii 'There are . . . . . . distant future' (ll. 38–40)
  iii 'Historians . . . . . . civilization' (ll. 50–52)
  iv 'In the case . . . . . . world' (ll. 56–8)

A i and ii only
B i and iii only
C i and iv only
D ii and iii only
E iii and iv only

6 The most important idea in ll. 30–36 is that

A important historic remains can only be preserved by rich governments or individuals

B important railway relics can be preserved by a wide variety of individuals

    C the kinds of relics that can be preserved from the railways are very various in nature

    D British railways have begun to see more clearly the need to preserve relics of their past

    E it is surprising what things appeal to nostalgic collectors

7 'Transition' (l. 25) means

    A adjustment
    B improvement
    C development
    D progress
    E change

8 'Boom' (l. 43) means

    A a steady rise in popularity
    B a sudden expansion in building and prosperity
    C an artificial inflation in value
    D a development of steam locomotives that made the world noisier
    E a rapid growth in popularity

9 'Valid' (l. 52) means

    A credible
    B authoritative
    C sound
    D possible
    E persuasive

10 The word 'devotees' (l. 57) suggests that for enthusiasts railways are a kind of

    A madness
    B hobby
    C obsession
    D religion
    E love-affair

From Section B

11 Which ONE of the following points about collecting railway relics is *not* mentioned in Section B?

    A ultimately one needs to collect only selected examples
    B it is human nature to begin by collecting a great variety of things
    C it is becoming increasingly difficult for the private collector to find railway relics
    D some items are suitable for display in a room in a house or club
    E one is limited in what one can collect by the storage space available

12 The literal meaning of 'cull out' (l. 6) is to

    A refrigerate fruit that is becoming overripe

  B kill an inferior animal
  C sprinkle water on vegetables that are losing their freshness
  D retain an animal for breeding purposes
  E fatten up an animal

13 In its context in l. 6 the metaphorical or figurative meaning of 'cull out' is to

  A put less value on
  B select for exclusion
  C ignore the existence of
  D remove to a different classification
  E put on display

14 Which ONE of the following phrases does *not* suggest that one should collect only certain types of railway relic?

  A 'definite aims' (l.2)
  B 'to be highly specialized' (l. 3)
  C 'a piecemeal assortment' (l. 4)
  D 'items of particular significance' (l. 7)
  E 'a pattern of development clearly defined' (ll. 8–9)

15 'Coherence' (l. 5) means

  A connection with one another
  B historical importance
  C appeal to enthusiasts
  D logical consistency
  E local or personal associations

From Section C

16 Section C classifies models in four categories as follows. In which TWO of them was their appearance very important?

  i the toy models mentioned in the first paragraph
  ii the scale models mentioned in the second paragraph
  iii the working models mentioned in the third paragraph
  iv the models of many sizes mentioned in the fourth paragraph

  A i and ii only
  B i and iii only
  C i and iv only
  D ii and iii only
  E ii and iv only

17 'Renaissance' (l. 2) means

  A popularity
  B revival
  C expansion
  D elaboration
  E restoration

18 The phrase 'is frequently the prelude to operations' (ll. 16–17) means
    that the collecting of railway relics often

    A is a cheap substitute for having working models
    B creates the desire to have working models
    C leads on to having working models
    D is inferior to having working models
    E is a necessary first step before having working models

19 'Doyen' (l. 33) means

    A senior member
    B founder
    C expert
    D favourite
    E darling

20 'The potential of the home market' (ll. 39–40) means

    A the expansion of the home market
    B the patriotic appeal of modelling only British railways
    C the number of models that could possibly be sold in the future in
       Britain
    D the profitability of selling model railways in Britain
    E the comparative ease of selling model railways in Britain

22 A word that is used in a slightly colloquial way is

    A 'layout' (l. 23)
    B 'microscopic' (l. 26)
    C 'stocked' (l. 30)
    D 'apprenticed' (l. 34)
    E 'atrocious' (l. 49)

TRADITIONAL QUESTIONS

Answer the following questions in your own words as far as possible.
Questions marked with an asterisk should be answered *very briefly*, and in
these answers complete sentences are not necessary.

From Section A

*1 Give in a single word or short phrase the meaning of *five* of the fol-
    lowing words *as used in the passage*:

    i paradox (l.8)   ii preservation (l.11)   iii transition (l.25)
    iv environment (l.26)   v scope (l.38)   vi schedule (l.41)
    vii scrapped (l.47).

2 Explain in your own words what is the paradox referred to in line 8.

3 Comment on the use of the words 'challenge' (l. 10) and 'launched'
   (l. 11).

4 What do you understand by the phrase 'nostalgic and sentimental'
   (l. 23)?

5 What is the difference, according to the writer, between preserving 'railwayana' and objects such as valuable paintings and tapestries?

6 What helps to make railway relics available to the public?

7 According to historians, what is the importance of preserving railway relics?

8 Give in your own words the meaning of the sentence 'The need and interest . . . . . . reasonable analysis' (ll. 54–6).

From Section B

*9 Give in a single word or short phrase the meaning of *five* of the following words *as used in the passage*:

i specialized (l. 3) ii piecemeal (l. 4) iii coherence (l. 5) iv cull (l. 6) v décor (l. 23) vi theme (l. 24).

10 Explain the expression 'a pattern of development clearly defined by objectives and limitations' (ll. 8–9).

11 What are the limitations to a collection of railwayana mentioned by the writer?

12 Besides their interest as a collection, what other purpose may items of railway equipment serve?

From Section C

*13 Give in a single word or short phrase the meaning of *five* of the following words *as used in the passage*:

i renaissance (l. 2) ii acquisition (l. 9) iii trends (l. 10) iv haberdashers (l. 32) v doyen (l. 33) vi components (l. 36) vii prototypes (l. 41).

14 What is the collection of model engines and railway accessories usually the prelude to, according to the writer?

15 Why are the windows of chemists and haberdashers called 'unlikely' (l. 31)?

16 Explain the expression 'Bassett-Lowke models became a household name' (l. 42).

17 Put into your own words the last sentence 'Compared with . . . . . . a solution' (ll. 47–51).

II. Writing English

Write on ONE of the following:

a Is it too late to revive the railways?

b Describe a train journey you have made during which every kind of mishap you can think of occurred.

c A visit to a transport or railway museum.

d A story entitled 'The Ghost Train'.

e Superstitions.

f The Pilgrims' Way.

g A coincidence.

h Battered babies.

i Write a story, a description or an essay suggested by the illustration above. (Your composition may be directly about the subject of the illustration, or may only take suggestions from it, but there must be some clear connection between the illustration and the composition.)

Suggestions for Projects, Assignments and Course Work

1 Make a study of the newspaper. You could trace the history of newspapers, or consider today's national and local papers. What do you expect from newspapers, and what do you get? Compare the treatment of the same item of political news in two different papers e.g. in *The Daily Mail* and *The Daily Mirror*. Compare the contents of such papers as *The Times* and *The Sun*. Find out the meanings of such expressions as 'free-lance', 'scoop', 'leader', and 'stop press'.

2 Choose any period in the past and compare its entertainments and

sports with those of today. For example, find out about the 18th-century gladiators, cockfighting, bull baiting, and the pleasure gardens of Vauxhall and Ranelagh. Study all aspects—players, spectators, finances.

III. Using English

Punctuation

1 Account for the following marks of punctuation in the passage of Part I:

i the dashes before 'according' and after 'outlook' (l.A. 23)   **ii** the commas before and after 'however' (l.A. 27)   **iii** the commas before 'judging' (l.B. 10) and after 'trends' (l.B. 10)   **iv** the comma after 'artistic' (l.B. 25)   **v** the dashes before 'made' (l.C. 44) and after 'standards' (l.C. 45).

2 Combine the following sentences into one long sentence, using 'and' and 'but' as little as possible:

It was the White Rabbit. It trotted slowly back again. The White Rabbit was looking anxiously about. It seemed to have lost something. Alice heard it muttering to itself. She guessed it was looking for the fan. She very good-naturedly began hunting for it. It was nowhere to be seen.

Grammar and Usage

3 Use each of the following expressions in separate sentences so as to bring out clearly the meaning of the expressions:

i Hobson's choice   **ii** the last straw   **iii** swan song   **iv** a fish out of water   **v** mushroom growth.

4 Use the following words in separate sentences so as to bring out the differences in meaning:

i dignified   **ii** imperious   **iii** disdainful   **iv** scornful   **v** insolent.

Spelling and Dictionary Work

5 Find out the derivation of the following words:

i bedlam   **ii** ferret   **iii** monk   **iv** parachute   **v** pantry
vi whisky   **vii** sherry   **viii** cider   **ix** port (drink)   **x** brandy
xi coffee.

6 The following words are incomplete. The dots indicate a letter or letters missing. The number of dots bears no relationship to the number of letters missing. Write out the words, spelling them correctly.

i tomat . . . . s   **ii** umb . . . . ella   **iii** quarre . . . . ing
iv develop . . . . ent   **v** hum . . . . rist   **vi** wilfu . . . . (headstrong)
vii n . . . . ther (of two alternatives)   **viii** n . . . . ce (brother's daughter)
ix pit . . . . ful   **x** gramm . . . . r.

Style and Appreciation

7 The following poem by Stella Gibbons is called 'Africa'.

> Cloudless and regal burns the day
> Over the sands of Africa.
>
> Parrots curl their golden feet
> Round ebony boughs, and drink the heat,
> While the lizard sees, from his limestone ledge,
> The burnt air dance at the precipice edge.
>
> Four thousand feet in the sky's pale arch
> The lazy armies of clouds march;
> Four thousand feet in the plain below
> Straw huts drowse, and the stream winds slow.
>
> Lilies and crocodiles flower in the mud,
> And teak logs spin in the wayward flood.
>
> Like noon's own spirit burns the day
> Over the beaches of Africa.

  i Show how the poet produces the impression of heat in the poem.
 ii What is the effect of repetition?
iii Explain the meaning of line 11 ('Lilies and crocodiles . . . . .')
 iv Pick out three metaphors and show how they are more effective
     than plain statements.
  v The title is 'Africa'. What is the theme?

Books to read

Nightrunners of Bengal	John Masters
The Living Desert	Walt Disney
No Room in the Ark	Alan Moorehead
Forbidden Jungle	Ross Salmon
The Lost World of the Kalahari	Laurens van der Post
Operation Noah	Charles Lagus
Short Stories	Stuart Cloete
Machineries of Joy	Ray Bradbury
The Thirty-Nine Steps	John Buchan
Highland River	Neil M. Gunn

Additional Exercises

1

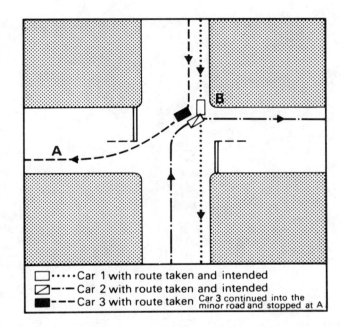

□ ·····Car 1 with route taken and intended
◨ —·—Car 2 with route taken and intended
■ ———Car 3 with route taken Car 3 continued into the minor road and stopped at A

All three cars were in the positions shown at the time of the colli-
sion. Cars 1 and 2 collided as shown and remained in this position.
Make reports of the accident from the point of view of

i the driver of car 1   **ii** the driver of car 2   **iii** a passenger in the
rear seat of car 3   **iv** a pedestrian standing at B   **v** a policeman
called to the accident. Be careful to make your reports typical of
the characters. For example, few motorists regard themselves as
responsible for accidents. In conclusion, give your own views of
the cause of the accident and apportion the blame.

* Remember that reports **i** to **iv** are by ordinary members of the
public who were present when the accident happened. Report **v** is
by a policeman, who arrived later, but he has been trained to
observe and to make exact and detailed reports of accidents.

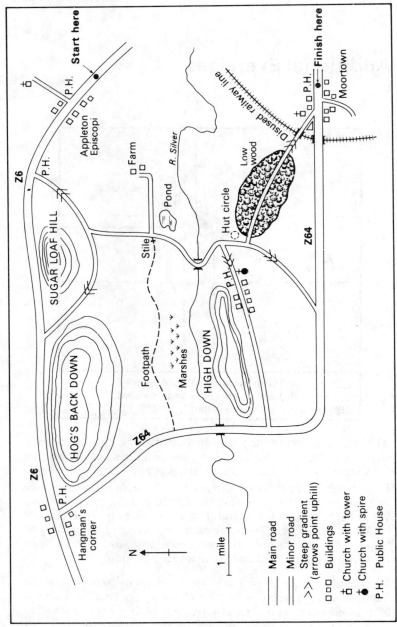

Start here

Finish here

P.H.

Moortown

Disused railway line

Low wood

Z6

P.H.

Appleton
Episcopi

R. Silver

Hut circle

P.H.

Farm

Pond

Z64

SUGAR LOAF HILL

Stile

P.H.

Footpath

HIGH DOWN

HOG'S BACK DOWN

Marshes

Z64

Z6

P.H.

Hangman's
corner

N

1 mile

————— Main road

══════ Minor road

>> Steep gradient
    (arrows point uphill)

□□□ Buildings

⌖ Church with tower

● Church with spire

P.H. Public House

2 A hiker is on the main road. Z6, south-east of Appleton Episcopi, at the spot marked 'Start here'. Give directions for walking to Moortown, by the shortest route along minor roads, leaving the Z6 by the first possible road. Describe the landmarks the hiker will see on his way, making use of all the details shown on the sketch-map which would be of help to the hiker in finding his way.

3 Study the table on pages 182–183 and then answer the questions.

   i Choose the zips which are likely to give the longest service despite frequent laundering.

   ii If in addition to the above quality you need the greatest variety of length and colour you can buy, which zip would you buy?

   iii Which zip would you choose if you were considering only ease of fitting and cheapness?

   iv Which zip under 18 pence per length tested is likely to give the longest service?

   v Which zip seems least satisfactory from the following points of view: little choice of colour, high price, and laundering?

   vi Choose the metal zip which is outstanding for cheapness and variety of colours available.

4 Study the table on pages 184–5 and then answer the questions.

   i Choose the best resorts for young people who want good beaches and swimming facilities, together with entertainment at night.

   ii Which resort are older people who want a wide choice of sporting activities and excursions likely to choose, especially if expense is no object?

   iii Some resorts are served by many tour operators. Choose the six most popular with tour operators and select from these six the cheapest holiday which is likely to satisfy family parties.

   iv Which resort would suit those who want a beautiful setting together with the best excursions?

   v Which resort is least suitable for older people who are interested in swimming and sporting activities?

   vi Choose the resort which offers the most expensive holiday. In what ways is it superior in general facilities to the cheapest resort, and in what ways is it inferior?

5 *Ambiguities*
The following sentences are badly expressed. Try to rewrite the sentences as you think the original writer intended to write them in order to convey his real meaning.

   a He has discovered a way of possibly staying the ageing process, which he describes as a reversible disease. His discovery could take years off your life.

   b When I make out my income-tax, can I take off my clothes?

(*Continued on page 186.*)

ZIPS

KEY: THE MORE BLOBS THE BETTER

	teeth made from	lengths available inches	number of colours	length tested inches	price of length tested (p)	durability	laundering	sewing in
ULTRA-LIGHT								
Aero blue pack	metal	4 to 10 × 1 12 to 24 × 2	47	10	17	●	● ● ●	● ● ●
Aeroluxe—tagged	polyester	4 to 10 × 1 12 to 24 × 2	42	8	17	● ● ● ●	● ● ●	● ● ●
Lightning black pack	metal	4 to 10 × 1 12 to 26 × 2	40	8	14½	● ● ● ●	●	not tested
LIGHT								
Aero orange pack	metal	6, 7, 8, 9	47	8	14½	● ●	● ● ●	● ● ●
Aero Zephyr—tagged	nylon	4 to 10 × 1 12 to 24 × 2	42	8	13	● ●	●	● ● ●
Lightning red/black pack	metal	6, 7, 8, 9	27	8	14½	● ● ● ●	● ●	●
Lightning-Zipp—tagged	nylon	4 to 8 × 1 10 to 24 × 2	60	8	14½	● ●	● ● ●	● ●
Opti-lon red pack	nylon	4 to 10 × 1 12 to 26 × 2	61	8	16½	● ● ● ●	● ● ●	●

	teeth made from	lengths available inches	number of colours	length tested inches	price of length tested (p)	durability	laundering	sewing in
Opti-matic—tagged	nylon	4 to 8 × 2 cm 10 to 24 × 5 cm	60	8	14½	●●●●	●●●	●●●
Pikaby Nylon—tagged	nylon	4, 6, 7, 8 to 22 × 2	72	8	14	●●●●	●●●●	●●●
YKK—tagged	nylon	4 to 10 × 1 12 to 24 × 2	60	8	13	●●●●●	●●●	●●●
MEDIUM								
Aero green pack	metal	12 to 26 × 2	19	12	21	●●●●●	●●	●●
Opti-lon blue pack	polyester	10 to 26 × 2	25	10	24	●●●●●	●●●	●●
MEDIUM-HEAVY								
Lightning orange pack	metal	8, 9, 10, 11, 12	3	8	22	●●●	●	●
CONCEALED INVISIBLE								
Lightning purple pack	polyester	8 and 9	17	8	18½	●●●	●●●●	●●●
Opti-lon orange pack	polyester	8 and 9	14	8	18½	●●●●	●●●	●●●
Pikaby Alco—light	metal	12, 18, 20, 22	14	12	27	●●	●●	●●●
Pikaby Alco—medium	metal	8 only	14	8	20	●	●●	●●●

ZIPS from *Which?* July 1973. (Consumers' Association)

RESORTS	tour operators	price range 14 nights in August (adults)	MEMBERS' RATING setting	beaches	swimming
COSTA BRAVA					
Calella de Palafrugel	H	£61	••	••	•
Estartit	ACHP	£53 to £62	•••	•••	••••
Lloret de Mar	ABCFGHKL PSTXY	£42 to £48	•	••	•
Rosas	AY	£43 to £77	••	•••	•••
Tossa de Mar	ACGKLPXY	£44 to £105	•••	••	•
COSTA DORADA					
Calella de la Costa	BCFGHKLPS TXY	£41 to £98	•	••	•
Salou	BHKLT	£46 to £59	••	•••	••••
Santa Susana	BKTY	£45 to £53	•	••	•
Sitges	AGLTX	£52 to £151	•••	•••	•••
Tarragona	A	£57 to £81	••	••	••
COSTA BLANCA					
Benidorm	ABCFGHK LPSTXY	£43 to £133	••	••••	•••
COSTA DEL SOL					
Fuengirola	FGLSX	£71 to £99	••	••	••
Marbella	ACFGHKPSTX	£63 to £189	••	••	••
Torremolinos	ABCFGHK LPSTX	£61 to £166	•	••	••
MAJORCA					
Alcudia	BGKPSTX	£50 to £72	••	••	•••
Arenal	ABCFGHK PSTXY	£50 to £126	•	••	•••
Cala Millor	BGHKLPST	£49 to £70	••	•••	•••
Cala Ratjada	ACFGHKLX	£51 to £76	•••	••	••
C'an Pastilla	ABCGHLPSTX	£52 to £126	••	••	••
C'an Picafort	BCFGKTY	£51 to £64	••	•••	••
Magalluf	AFGHKPSTX	£57 to £118	•	••	••
Palma	ACGHLPSTX	£57 to £124	•••	•	••
Palma Nova	AFGHKLPSTX	£56 to £118	••	••	•••
Paguera	AFHLPX	£53 to £99	••	••	•••
IBIZA					
Playa d'en Bossa	HTY	£55 to £62	•	••	••
Es Cana	BFGHKY	£53 to £77	••	••	••
Figueretes	HKT	£53 to £70	••	•	••
San Antonio Abad	ABCFGHKL PSTX	£51 to £94	••	•	••
Santa Eulalia de Rio	ACHKTX	£48 to £94	•••	•	••
Portinatx	FT	£54 to £64	•••	•••	••••

KEY: THE MORE BLOBS THE BETTER

MEMBERS' OVERALL RATING

sporting activities	excursions	night life	family parties	older people	younger people	
						COSTA BRAVA
●●	●●	●●	●●	●●	●●	Calella de Palafrugel
●●●●	●●	●●●	●●●	●●	●●	Estartit
●●	●●	●●●●	●	●	●●●●	Lloret de Mar
●●	●●	●●	●●●	●●	●●	Rosas
●●	●●●	●●●	●	●●	●●	Tossa de Mar
						COSTA DORADA
●	●●	●●●	●	●	●●●	Calella de la Costa
●●	●	●●	●●●	●●	●●	Salou
●	●●	●●	●●	●●	●●	Santa Susana
●●●	●●	●●●	●●	●	●●●	Sitges
●●	●●	●●	●●	●●	●●	Tarragona
						COSTA BLANCA
●●●	●●	●●●●	●●●	●	●●●●	Benidorm
						COSTA DEL SOL
●●	●●	●●	●●	●●	●●	Fuengirola
●●●●	●●●	●●	●●	●●●	●●	Marbella
●●●●	●●●	●●●	●	●	●●●	Torremolinos
						MAJORCA
●	●	●	●●	●●	●	Alcudia
●●●	●●	●●●	●●	●	●●●	Arenal
●●	●●	●●	●●●	●●	●●	Cala Millor
●●	●●	●●	●●	●●	●●	Cala Ratjada
●●	●●	●●	●●	●●	●●●	C'an Pastilla
●●	●●	●●	●●●	●●	●●	C'an Picafort
●●	●	●●●	●●	●●	●●	Magalluf
●●●	●●●●	●●●	●	●●	●●	Palma
●●	●●●	●●	●●●	●●	●●	Palma Nova
●●	●●	●●	●●	●●	●●	Paguera
						IBIZA
●●	●	●	●●●	●●	●	Playa d'en Bossa
●●	●●	●	●●●	●	●●	Es Cana
●	●●	●	●	●●	●●	Figueretes
●●	●●	●●●	●●	●	●●●	San Antonio Abad
●●	●●	●	●	●●●	●	Santa Eulalia del Rio
	●●	●	●●●	●	●	Portinatx

Key: tour operators

A Apal	B Blue Sky	C Cosmos	F Flair/Hickie Borman	G Global
H Horizon	K Clarksons	L Lord Brothers	P Lunn Poly	S Sunair
T Thomson	Y Lyons	X Cooks		

HOLIDAYS IN SPAIN, From *Which?* January 1972, (Consumers' Association)

c How soon before they die do people have to pay their taxes?

d The teacher taught the Home Economics class how to cook, iron and serve a meal.

e I am forwarding my marriage certificate and my three children, one of which is a mistake.

6 In its way the following sentence, taken from advertising 'blurb', is equally puzzling. Can you produce a simpler version?

'The book will, we hope, be of interest to arts teachers because it suggests a hypothesis about ways in which the experience of the arts may be arranged in the curriculum so as to be given a sense of direction or a developmental sequence of increasing refinement related to the emotional maturation of adolescents.'

7 Show the difference in meaning between the expressions in the following pairs:

a a smoking jacket, a smoking-jacket;

b a singing master, a singing-master;

c a walking stick, a walking-stick;

d a rolling pin, a rolling-pin.

8 *Proverbial expressions*

Proverbs are figurative expressions, not to be taken literally, but conveying a general truth, or an example of one. The unfortunate plight of 'a fish out of water' needs little imagination. But it is more difficult to use the expression of a person who is in circumstances as disastrous as those of the fish.

Many proverbs give advice or warning. 'Make hay while the sun shines' is good literal advice, but it is normally taken to mean that you should do things at the right time and when the opportunity occurs.

Try to explain the meaning of the following foreign proverbs:

a Good bargains empty the purse;

b By a humble spark is a town set on fire;

c Better to be the head of a cat than the tail of a lion;

d Who has a head of wax must not come near the fire;

e A golden bit does not make a horse any better.

You should be able to think of English proverbs that convey a similar meaning to some of the above.

Note also that proverbs are frequently contradictory, e.g. 'Look before you leap' and 'He who hesitates is lost'; but in the right circumstances both proverbs can be true. The trouble is, who makes the decision about which proverb to apply?

9 *Compositions, Projects, Assignments and Course Work*

a Few workers today have any interest in the end-product of their labours; indeed, they rarely see it. This is the cause of strikes—lack of interest, monotony, and discontent with working conditions. Write a composition of five paragraphs, each beginning with a 'topic' sentence, i.e. a sentence that includes the main point of the paragraph, while the rest of the paragraph expands the information given in the first sentence.

b Is a 'drop-out' from society motivated by courage, cowardice, contempt, or moral superiority?

c If you could choose, would you like to live in the country or in a town? Organize your answer clearly into advantages and disadvantages, saying what kind of town or what part of the country you would prefer.

d A night in the marshes.

e Imagine you are one of King Arthur's soldiers engaged in fighting against the Saxon invaders. Give an account of your adventures and hardships. Locate your actions in a suitable part of the country.

f Write a description of a fire you have actually seen, or a fire you have read about (see *The History of Mr Polly*).

g A short story entitled 'Money for Nothing'.

h 'It never rains but it pours.'

i The changing towns. Read John Betjeman's 'Lines written to Martyn Skinner before his departure from Oxfordshire in search of quiet—1961'.

j The pleasures of photography.

k Family rows. Read *Billy Liar*.

l You like or dislike detective stories. Write a letter to a friend who holds the opposite point of view and try to justify your own. Refer to detective stories you have read, films you have seen, or radio stories or plays to which you have listened.

m Write a description of a person, well known to you, who is wanted by the police. Include details of complexion and physique, clothing, habits, and possible disguises. Divide your description logically into paragraphs, e.g. physical characteristics, clothing, habits etc.

n Most people write about what they see. Good writers appeal to the other senses—of hearing, smell, touch and taste. Some are particularly good at describing movement. Write an account of a walk you take during a particular season of the year in the town, in the countryside, or by the sea, using the hints given above. Your composition should be about 450 words, and consist of four or five paragraphs, each dealing with a different aspect of your subject.

o Read through any five extracts used in this book and show the difference between title and theme.

p Science fiction books vary greatly in credibility. Mention **i** one book you have read in which you can believe in the characters and the incidents, and **ii** one book which you find unreal for one or more reasons. Write a full account of the book mentioned in **i** or **ii** above; plot, characters, setting, and dialogue should all be considered.

q When asked why he wanted to climb a mountain, a mountaineer replied, 'Because it's there.' What do you think about this philosophy of life?

r Write a letter to the manager of your local cinema or theatre praising or complaining about **i** the choice of programmes **ii** the consideration of the comfort of the audience—seating, smoking, air conditioning, refreshments **iii** the organization—reserving of seats, queuing outside or under cover.

s   How to make a model of a theatre, a sports stadium, or a stretch of countryside for a school exhibition. Give full details from the beginning when you decide on the scale and the materials to be used.

t   Choose a book (a story or a play) in which the main character is faced with a problem. Describe the character, the problem, and the solution, if there was one.

u   Write in diary form the account of an expedition which has just returned from exploring a little-known part of the world.

v   Which would you prefer—a job which is well paid and adventurous, or one which is safe but relatively poorly paid? Consider not only the next few years when you are young, but also the future with its inevitable responsibilities.

w   Every year fires cause loss of life and destruction of property. If you had the power, what steps would you take to reduce the number of fires? Think about the precautions necessary for industrial as well as domestic premises.

x   Describe a scene connected with one of the following: **i** a Rag Day   **ii** a local Carnival   **iii** a procession   **iv** a Wakes Week celebration.

10 *Short exercises*

A *Definitions*
Give brief definitions of five of the following:

i a table   **ii** a teapot   **iii** a ladder   **iv** a newspaper
v a window   **vi** a dictionary   **vii** an axe   **viii** a corkscrew
ix a lighthouse.

It is useful in describing objects in detail to remember certain points:
a Shape   **b** Use   **c** Material   **d** Size   [the initials spell SUMS].

There are also useful words which can be employed to avoid the word 'thing', such as: article, object, receptacle, utensil, tool, instrument, implement, container.

B *Short essays*
Write about 200 words on TWO of the following subjects:

i At the hairdresser's   **ii** Young people owe their parents nothing
iii Loneliness   **iv** The lies people tell.

C *Short essays*
Write about 200 words on TWO of the following subjects:

i Cleaning and care of an electric or gas cooker   **ii** How to darn a pair of socks   **iii** Maintaining a bicycle   **iv** How to fit a new washer to a cold-water tap   **v** What can we tell about people from the clothes they wear?   **vi** Giving first aid to someone who has received an electric shock   **vii** Painting a new pair of garage doors   **viii** What do you think about 'demonstrations'?

D *Descriptive essays*

Write a short essay (about 250 words) suggested by one of the following:

i	'This is the season when a few Dry leaves hang on dry wood.'
ii	'A shadow is floating through the moonlight. Its wings don't make a sound.'
iii	'Lord: it is Time. The summer was so good. Now lay your shadows on the sundial's face.'
iv	'Dark of primaeval pine encircles me With distant thunder of an angry sea.'
v	'Mountains are moving, rivers are hurrying. But we are still.'
vi	'The train. A hot July. On either hand Our sober, fruitful, unemphatic land.'
vii	'Now is the time for the burning of the leaves.'
viii	'Into many a green valley Drifts the appalling snow.'
ix	'Between the railway and the mine, Brambles are in fruit again.'
x	'I climbed through woods in the hour-before-dawn dark. Evil air, a frost-making stillness.'

Appendix

READING WITH A PURPOSE

If you are taking an examination you are reading, we hope, with pleasure and with a purpose. It is as well to prepare yourself by making up your mind about your books before you take the examination. Have you read about characters who seem to resemble you? Can you think of characters between whom there is a conflict? What unpleasant characters have you read about? What particular qualities do certain characters show? Are they brave, arrogant, friendly, spiteful? Are the men better portrayed than the women? What qualities do you expect of a hero or heroine?

Be prepared to pick out incidents from fiction or non-fiction books which illustrate certain qualities in characters.

Make up your mind about the general qualities of the books you have read. Are they 'impossible to put down', and if so, why? Have some books changed your views about certain people and aspects of life? Are some books written not only to give pleasure but also, in your opinion, to teach or reform? Why is it that books dealing with everyday life are sometimes as exciting as 'incredible' adventure stories?

I. FICTION

When you have read a book you will probably be asked to talk about it or to write an appreciation of it. You may find this difficult unless you organize your thoughts. What you have to say could be arranged under three headings: plot, characters, and setting. Your remarks so arranged could indicate to a prospective reader what to expect. They will also convince anyone reading your work that you know what you are talking about.

Plot

Does the story hold your interest from the start? Are the events exciting? Do they proceed naturally, step by step, each episode contributing to the suspense (if there is any!) until the final climax, the scene in which all is explained and—if it is that kind of book—you realize that the characters will live happily ever after?

Characters

The characters are, or should be, inseparable from the plot. Do they, because they are what they are, influence the events which form the plot? Are they true to life? Are they consistent in themselves? Do they grow or change, as we do, as the result of circumstances and events? Are they merely puppets manipulated to suit the events?

Setting

However interesting the story and credible the characters, if the setting or background is ignored or inaccurate, the book will fail. The writer must create the right atmosphere, geographical and/or historical, if we are to achieve that 'suspension of disbelief' which will enable us to enter the world of the author and his people. The speech of the characters forms part of the setting, as well as indicating qualities of character. Too much regional or local dialect, and too much pseudo-historical speech is distracting; occasional hints are usually enough to convince the reader.

II. NON-FICTION

Some non-fiction books may be dealt with in much the same way as fiction books; but others may have a series of events which can hardly be called a plot. Some books tell about animals instead of people. It may therefore be more suitable to start an appreciation of a non-fiction book by dealing first with the subject matter. Decide whether the book can be called a travel book, a biography or autobiography, or a kind of reference book in which facts are presented in an interesting way. When you have decided what sort of book you are going to describe, summarize the information given in it and say how the writer makes his subject interesting. Your account should say whether the book is written in a style easy to understand, or in a style which has so many scientific terms, for example, that the non-specialist would find it difficult.

Always remember that you are trying to give enough information about your book to persuade someone to read—or not to read—it.

III. POETRY

Many examinations include questions which require a knowledge of selected poems and/or interpretation of 'unseen' poems. Obviously your English course will include reading and possibly memorizing poetry. Many readers of verse start by using anthologies which contain selections of work by many different poets, and then proceed to the study of the writings of particular poets whose style and opinions appeal to them. As in prose comprehension, the first task in the interpretation of a poem is to find out what the poet is saying. This can only be done by careful and possibly repeated reading. Once you have understood what is being said, you can proceed to the style—imagery (see Unit I, Part III, 6), diction (choice of words), metre—rhyme and rhythm. Finally try to assess the poet's intention. Is he merely describing? Is he trying to convert you to his point of view? Is he ridiculing people or institutions? What is his mood? Try to unite your opinions of content and style in your final appreciation.

Finally, keep in mind the following remarks made by modern poets:
'My verse is made to be said out loud. I regard verse as the shortest and most memorable way of saying things.' (John Betjeman)
'A poem communicates to every single reader individually.' (Patric Dickinson).
'Different readers see different things in a poem according to their experiences and temperaments. One might almost say that a poem has as many meanings as it has readers.' (Clifford Dyment)
'What a poem "means" is something that the writer as well as the reader

each must decide alone. Only one thing is certain: that, unlike arithmetic, the correct answers may all be right, yet all be different.' (Charles Causley)

To assist you to organize your poetry reading we have included below lists of topics which recur in examinations. This is not a 'spot the question' technique, but should help to prevent a completely haphazard approach.

Section 1 Poems dealing with particular themes.
Ships and the sea; the seasons; love; animals; war; death; birds; patriotism; travel; weather; nature; people; unusual subjects.

Section 2 Poems of a particular type.
Poems which are suitable for reading aloud/suitable for reading to oneself; are suitable for Morning Assembly; are suitable/unsuitable for use at Christmas or on Greetings cards; are likely to appeal to teenagers; are suitable for reciting round a camp fire. Some poems may have influenced your own writing of poetry.

Section 3 Poems having certain qualities.
Excitement; serenity; sadness; beauty of description; rhythm; humour; imagery.

Section 4 Miscellaneous topics.
Interests of the poet; how effects are achieved; why you like/dislike poetry; comparison/contrast of two poets (interests, attitudes, emotions); comparison/contrast of two poems (subject matter, style).

The following anthologies have been found suitable for use with G.C.E. and C.S.E. candidates in the Fourth and Fifth Years of a Secondary course: *Poems of Spirit and Action* (Arnold); *Dawn and Dusk* (Brockhampton); *Rhyme and Reason* (Chatto); *Albemarle Book of Modern Verse 1 & 11* (Murray); *Poets of Our Time* (Murray); *Poems of the Sixties* (Murray); *Every Man Will Shout* (Oxford University Press); *Voices* (Penguin); *1914–18 in Poetry* (University of London Press).

The following terms help you to talk about poetry. Find out what they mean from a dictionary or suitable reference book such as the *Oxford Companion to English Literature*.

Lyric, ballad, narrative, blank verse, sonnet, limerick, stanza, ode, elegy, metre, assonance, alliteration, echoism or onomatopoeia, subjective, objective.

BOOK LIST ARRANGED ACCORDING TO SUBJECT MATTER

Many of the books in the following list are included in the lists of books to read provided in each Unit, but in the Units the 'Books to Read' are a 'mixed bag'. Some of them are related in subject matter to the passage in Part I of the Unit; others are deliberately included to cover a wide range of interests. The following list will help the reader to choose similar books to those he has found worth while.

SCIENCE FICTION

The Best S.F. Stories of Brian Aldiss	
The Golden Apples of the Sun (short stories)	Ray Bradbury
Fahrenheit 451	Ray Bradbury
Timeless Stories for Today and Tomorrow	Ray Bradbury
The Death of Grass	John Christopher
Fall of Moondust	Arthur C. Clarke
Aspects of Science Fiction (short stories)	ed. G. D. Doherty
Second Orbit (short stories)	ed. G. D. Doherty
The Black Cloud	Fred Hoyle
Brave New World	Aldous Huxley
Out of the Silent Planet; Voyage to Venus	C. S. Lewis
Quatermass and the Pit	Nigel Kneale
1984	George Orwell
The War of the Worlds	H. G. Wells
The Day of the Triffids	John Wyndham
The Kraken Wakes	John Wyndham
The Trouble with Lichen	John Wyndham
The Seeds of Time (short stories)	John Wyndham

CRIME AND DETECTION

The Case of the Late Pig	Margery Allingham
The Incredulity of Father Brown	G. K. Chesterton
The Innocence of Father Brown	G. K. Chesterton
The Wisdom of Father Brown	G. K. Chesterton
Poirot Investigates	Agatha Christie
Sherlock Holmes Stories	A. Conan Doyle
Five Red Herrings; Hangman's Holiday	Dorothy L. Sayers
My Friend Maigret	Georges Simenon
The Eustace Diamonds	Anthony Trollope

ANIMALS

Zoo Quest to Guiana	David Attenborough
Man-Eaters of Kumaon	Jim Corbett
The Overloaded Ark	Gerald Durrell
The Bafut Beagles	Gerald Durrell
Seal Morning	Rosemary Farr
The Snow Goose	Paul Gallico
The Call of the Wild; White Fang	Jack London
Ring of Bright Water	Gavin Maxwell
The Otter's Tale	Gavin Maxwell
In Quest of a Mermaid	J. H. Williams
Tarka the Otter	Henry Williamson

TRAVEL AND ADVENTURE

Fair Stood the Wind for France	H. E. Bates
The Jacaranda Tree	H. E. Bates
The Thirty-Nine Steps	John Buchan
Greenmantle	John Buchan
Desperate Voyage	John Caldwell

The Jungle is Neutral	F. S. Chapman
Living Dangerously	F. S. Chapman
The Lost World	A. Conan Doyle
Three Singles to Adventure	Gerald Durrell
Moonfleet	J. M. Faulkner
The Hornblower Stories	C. S. Forester
A Pattern of Islands	Arthur Grimble
The Kon-Tiki Expedition	Thor Heyerdahl
Aku-Aku	Thor Heyerdahl
The White South	Hammond Innes
To Kill a Mockingbird	Harper Lee
Where Eagles Dare	Alistair MacLean
Walkabout	J. V. Marshall
South Col	Wilfrid Noyce
A Town Like Alice	Nevil Shute
Trustee from the Toolroom	Nevil Shute
The Hobbit	J. R. R. Tolkien
Huckleberry Finn	Mark Twain

GROWING UP

Lorna Doone	R. D. Blackmore
Lord of the Flies	William Golding
Old Yeller	F. Jipson
Cider with Rosie	Laurie Lee
The Catcher in the Rye	J. D. Salinger
Memoirs of a Foxhunting Man	Siegfried Sassoon
Billy Liar	Keith Waterhouse

WAR

Death of a Hero	Richard Aldington
The Dam Busters	Paul Brickhill
Colditz: The German Story	R. Eggers
Enemy Coast Ahead	Guy Gibson
Goodbye to All That	Robert Graves
The Good Soldier Schweik	Jaroslav Hasek
For Whom the Bell Tolls	Ernest Hemingway
The Man Who Never Was	Ewan Montague
The Colditz Story	P. R. Reid
Memoirs of an Infantry Officer	Siegfried Sassoon
The Tunnel	Eric Williams
The Wooden Horse	Eric Williams
One of Our Submarines	Edward Young

'THE BAD OLD DAYS'

The Stars Look Down	A. J. Cronin
Aneurin Bevan	Michael Foot
Love on the Dole	Walter Greenwood
Bidden to the Feast	Jack Jones
How Green was My Valley	Richard Llewellyn

The Road to Wigan Pier	George Orwell
Down and Out in Paris and London	George Orwell
English Journey	J. B. Priestley
Fame is the Spur	Howard Spring
Lark Rise to Candleford	Flora Thompson

THE SEA

The Bombard Story	Alain Bombard
Desperate Voyage	John Caldwell
The Silent World	J-Y Cousteau
Typhoon	Joseph Conrad
The Kon-Tiki Expedition	Thor Heyerdahl
In Hazard	Richard Hughes
The Cruel Sea	Nicholas Monsarrat
The 'Caine' Mutiny	Herman Wouk

COLOUR PREJUDICE

The Fire Next Time	James Baldwin
To Sir, With Love	E. R. Braithwaite
Naught for Your Comfort	Trevor Huddlestone
Cry, the Beloved Country	Alan Paton
Black and White	John Taylor
Black Boy	Richard Wright

'LUCKY DIP'

Lucky Jim	Kingsley Amis
Jane Eyre	Charlotte Brontë
Wuthering Heights	Emily Brontë
Clochemerle	Gabriel Chevallier
Funeral in Berlin	Len Deighton
One Pair of Feet	Monica Dickens
One Pair of Hands	Monica Dickens
Jamaica Inn	Daphne du Maurier
The African Queen	C. S. Forester
Brighton Rock	Graham Greene
The Mayor of Casterbridge	Thomas Hardy
A Farewell to Arms	Ernest Hemingway
Drayneflete Revealed	Osbert Lancaster
Nightrunners of Bengal	John Masters
Animal Farm	George Orwell
Parkinson's Law	C. Northcote Parkinson
The Good Companions	J. B. Priestley
The Grapes of Wrath	John Steinbeck
The History of Mr Polly	H. G. Wells
The Cry of a Bird	Dorothy Yglesias

SHORT STORIES BY

A. J. Alan, Isaac Asimov, J. G. Ballard, Stan Barstow, H. E. Bates,

Ambrose Bierce, Algernon Blackwood, Juanita Casey, G. K. Chesterton, Stuart Cloete, Jack Cope, A. E. Coppard, E. M. Forster, John Galsworthy, Thomas Hardy, W. W. Jacobs, Henry James, Rudyard Kipling, D. H. Lawrence, W. Somerset Maugham, Frank O'Connor, H. H. Munro ('Saki'), William Sansom, Muriel Spark, H. G. Wells, John Wyndham.

SHORT STORY ANTHOLOGIES
Aspects of the Short Story (John Murray)
Contact, Volumes I and II (John Murray)
Short Stories of Our Time (Harrap)
Short Stories (Longman's Modern Reading)
Short Stories of the 20th Century (Longman)
Story III (Penguin)

A LIST OF PLAYS

Antigone	Jean Anouilh
The Admirable Crichton	J. M. Barrie
The Caucasian Chalk Circle	Bertolt Brecht
Hobson's Choice	H. Brighouse
A Man for All Seasons	Robert Bolt
Plays of the Sixties	ed. J. M. Charlton
Murder in the Cathedral	T. S. Eliot
Four English Comedies (Penguin)	
A Sleep of Prisoners; The Dark is Light Enough; Curtmantle (O.U.P.)	Christopher Fry
Strife	John Galsworthy
Caste	John Galsworthy
The Government Inspector	Nikolai Gogol
Hedda Gabler etc (Penguin)	Henrik Ibsen
Rhineroceros etc (Penguin)	Eugene Ionesco
Doctor Faustus	Christopher Marlowe
The Crucible	Arthur Miller
Death of a Salesman	Arthur Miller
View from the Bridge	Arthur Miller
Noah	André Obey
Juno and the Paycock	Sean O'Casey
Look Back in Anger	John Osborne
Time and the Conways etc (Penguin)	J. B. Priestley
The Winslow Boy	Terence Rattigan
Macbeth	William Shakespeare
Androcles and the Lion	G. B. Shaw
Arms and the Man etc (Penguin)	G. B. Shaw
Pygmalion	G. B. Shaw
Saint Joan	G. B. Shaw
Journey's End	R. C. Sherriff
Zigger Zagger etc (Penguin)	Nick Terson
Under Milk Wood	Dylan Thomas

Three European Plays (Penguin) includes *The Queen and the Rebels*
Three Plays (Penguin) includes *The Long and the Short and the Tall*
Billy Liar   Keith Waterhouse & Willis Hall
Trilogy (Penguin)   Arnold Wesker
The Importance of Being Ernest   Oscar Wilde
Our Town   Thornton Wilder
The Matchmaker   Thornton Wilder

ORAL WORK: SUBJECTS FOR TALKS

Adolescence   Keeping a Pony
Aeromodelling
Airships and Balloons   Macrame
Archery   Making Pottery
                                  Making and Looking After an Aquarium
Ballet   Money
Bats   Mountaineering
Beds
Budgerigars   Nylon
Butterflies
                                  Oil
Camping   Olympic Games
Cars, Veteran and Vintage   Orienteering
Castles   Origami
Coarse Fishing
Collecting . . . .   Pebbles on the Beach
Communications Satellites   Photography
                                  Plastics
Dartmoor
Dinghy Sailing   Railway Modelling
Dinosaurs   Rugby
Dog Care
Dressmaking   Sailing
Drugs   Sea Fishing
                                  Sea Monsters
Elizabeth I   Shell Fish
                                  Skin and Scuba Diving
Falconry   Steam Traction Engines
First Aid   Surf Canoeing
Flower Arrangement
Freshwater Fishing   Trains

Gardening   Volcanoes

Hairdressing   Warships
Haunted Houses   Weather
House Plants
                                  Yoga
Judo

Index

Questions	Units														
	1	2	3	4	5	6	7	8	9	10	11	12	13	14	15
1	A	A	A	C	A	B	B	E	C	B	B	C	C	A	B
2	A	C	C	D	D	C	C	E	C	E	B	E	E	D	D
3	E	D	B	A	C	B	D	D	B	C	C	D	D	A	B
4	B	A	C	E	C	E	E	C	E	C	C	C	A	C	B
5	B	E	D	A	B	B	C	B	A	B	E	E	D	E	A
6	B	D	A	B	A	D	E	E	A	E	B	B	B	A	B
7	D	B	C	E	C	C	D	B	D	B	E	C	C	B	E
8	A	E	E	B	D	C	A	B	E	A	D	D	D	A	B
9	B	B	A	A	B	B	E	A	C	A	A	A	D	E	C
10	A	E	C	A	B	D	C	B	D	E	D	C	A	A	D
11	E	B	A	D	C	A	E	C	B	D	C	B	A	B	C
12	C	A	C	B	D	C	B	B	C	D	C	D	B	B	B
13	D	D	E	C	A	C	C	D	D	E	B	C	B	C	B
14	C	C	E	D	C	A	A	B	D	D	B	A	D	C	C
15	C	E	A	B	E	B	B	C	A	A	A	B	E	E	A
16	B	A	D	C	B	E	A	D	D	E	E	D	B	C	E
17	C	E	E	A	A	C	D	C	E	C	A	C	C	D	B
18	D	D	B	B	D	A	A	D	E	A	B	E	B	A	C
19	D	C	D	E	E	C	A	D	B	B	C	A	A	C	A
20	C	D	D	B	C	D	E	A	A	E	A	E	E	D	C
21	C	C	C		B	A	C	A	A		E	A	C	C	E
22	E	E			E	E	B	A				E		D	
23	E						E					C		B	
24												D			
25												B			